Weighing up the Evidence

TIMELINE:

Women and Power

Sue Mayfield

Dryad Press Limited London

Contents

Typeset by Tek-Art Ltd, Kent
and printed in Great Britain by
Anchor Brendon Ltd
Tiptree, Essex
for the Publishers
Dryad Press Limited,
8 Cavendish Square,
London W1M 0AJ

ISBN 0 8521 9768 3

ACKNOWLEDGMENTS

The author would like to thank the following for their help in the preparation of this book; Lyndall Gordon, Sarah Harris, Liz Knight, Keith Mallinson, Tim Mayfield, Iris Preston and Helen Spencer.

The author and publishers thank the following for their kind permission to reproduce copyright illustrations: His Grace the Archbishop of Canterbury, and the Trustees of Lambeth Palace Library, page 9; Bodleian Library, pages 31, 40; R.F. Brien, pages 43, 53; BBC Hulton Picture Library, page 27 (right); the British Library Board, pages 14, 24, 38; Cambridge University Press, page 5 (from Richard B. Lee, The !Kung San); Kip Crooks, pages 10, 21 (left); Committee of the Egypt Exploration Society, page 6; Mary Evans Picture Library, pages 25, 41; Imperial War Museum, page 45; Kevin Kallagher, page 50; Ms Jill Liddington, Lancashire Record Office, page 48; the Mansell Collection, page 15; by kind permission of the Marquess of Tavistock, and the Trustees of the Bedford Estates, Woburn Abbey, page 22; the National Gallery of Ireland, page 32; Österreichische Nationalbibliothek, Bildarchiv, page 16; Raissa Page/Format Photographers, page 52; Pierpont Morgan Library, New York, page 18; University of Reading, Institute of Agricultural History and Museum of English Rural Life, page 21 (right).

Front cover: Mary Evans Picture Library (top left and right).

Introduction

History is often seen as the stories of the lives of great men; a catalogue of the exploits of outstanding kings, warriors, and politicians. Until quite recently, little attention was given to the everyday lives of ordinary people, and even less was given to the lives of women. Many history books give the impression that for large parts of our past women did not exist!

This book will try to piece together a picture of women throughout history, looking specifically at the issue of power. Because of the large amount of material and the limitations of so short a book, I have concentrated on the British Isles. In many periods of British history, women were virtually absent from the realm of public, political power. It was not until 1918 that a woman was elected as a Member of Parliament. Traditionally, men have fought the battles, sat on the thrones, passed the laws, and made the important decisions.

Men have often justified this control over women, and their exclusion from positions of public power, by arguing that women are biologically, intellectually, or emotionally inferior to men. Aristotle believed that women were a "mistake" of Nature and that only men were the true image of the Divine. Martin Luther thought that men's broad shoulders made them intelligent, whereas women's broad hips made them well-suited to a lot of sitting down! The Victorian thinker John Ruskin maintained that a woman's intellect was better suited to home-making than to politics.

Some women were exceptions to this pattern and held power in essentially patriarchal, or male-dominated societies. Boudica, Elizabeth I, Queen Victoria, and, in the 1980s, Margaret Thatcher, are all examples of British women in power. Overseas, Indira Gandhi, Golda Meir, Joan of Arc and Sirimavo Bandaranaike are similar examples. Men have often, rather insultingly, likened such women to "men in female disguise", claiming that power is a masculine preserve and that to attain it, women must in some way become unfeminine — they must become honorary men. Such an understanding of women in power is, of course, unacceptably narrow and falls into the trap of seeing history as purely the lives of the outstanding, the "super people".

Power is not just about government and control. Ordinary people possess power of a different kind: they have influence — the ability to affect, or change, the lives of individuals, or groups of individuals, by example or pressure. At times in the past women had great influence on society's structures. In Anglo-Saxon times they owned and sold property, made enormous financial contributions to good works, and held considerable authority as Abbesses of great monasteries. In the Middle Ages women practised medicine, travelled abroad on pilgrimages and held prominent positions in some areas of religious life.

Women have conducted some very powerful campaigns for social changes. During the 1640s a large body of women lobbied Parliament after they had lost their livelihoods as a result of the Civil War. In the last century women were very active in the Trades Union movement and in fighting for their right to vote. Very recently, women have had enormous influence on both the peace movement and, in 1984, on the course of the miners' strike.

Many women who have no public power may nevertheless have great power within family units as wives and mothers. There are rarely records of power of this sort, and it is often difficult to pinpoint or to measure it. Some societies are essentially matricentric (centred around mothers) even though the men may have outward control and authority.

Women's unique ability to bear children and give birth, has often been greatly feared by men. Many cultures have traditional customs that have arisen – amongst other reasons – because of men's fear of menstruation and childbirth. In Europe in the Middle Ages, midwives were regarded with suspicion because of their part in the mysterious event of childbirth. Many were outlawed by the Church, which accused them of being witches and accomplices of the Devil.

This book will try to reconstruct the lives of women, focusing on their power and powerlessness. It will also pose and attempt to answer questions such as: What is power? Why have men traditionally held political power? Why have women at times in the past been denied access to resources and education? What social and economic factors limit and determine power?

The book is arranged in six time periods, in an attempt to show a pattern of the change and developments that have affected women's power and powerlessness. Change, of course, never occurs at a regular pace, nor has women's power either increased or decreased at a steady rate from ancient times to the present day. Women have gained or lost power at various times as a result of many varied social, economic, political and philosophical pressures.

The extent to which we can understand the lives of women is limited by the sources of evidence available to us. This inevitably results in a patchy and incomplete picture. The majority of our records, chronicles, diaries and history books have been written by men, and so they often fail to represent the ideas and experiences of the female section of the population. For many periods of the past, there is little written evidence of the lives of poor people, since it was generally the wealthy who had the leisure, education and resources to record events. In many situations, wealth equals power, and so powerlessness becomes linked with insignificance.

As you read you may come across words which are unfamiliar to you or that have changed their meaning through time. The glossary on pages 55-57 will help you to understand these. The *Timeline* on pages 61-63 will help you to put the evidence presented in chapters 1-6 into its wider historical context and to understand the social and economic changes that have affected the power of women.

Power is a difficult thing to describe and to measure, and the part played by women throughout British history has been too great and too multi-faceted to assess adequately within the space of this book. *Women and Power* is an attempt to begin to understand both the nature of power and the history of women. I hope that after having studied this book, you will have a greater awareness of the historical power of women.

Before 1066

PREHISTORIC BRITAIN

Virtually no written evidence exists to show us what the lives of people in Britain were like before the Roman invasion in 43 AD. Historians have studied archaeological remains and fossils in order to piece together a picture of how people lived, who did what and who had power, but their conclusions are limited and involve a lot of guesswork. How a society acquires, produces, or organizes its food supply has a major impact on its social arrangement and on the distribution of power and status.

The earliest prehistoric peoples probably obtained their food by hunting and gathering rather than as a result of an organized system of planting crops and rearing animals. Some researchers believe that by studying hunter-gatherer societies that still exist today in other parts of the world, we can find clues about the customs and lifestyles of prehistoric peoples in Britain.

THE !KUNG SAN HUNTER GATHERERS

The !Kung San are a group of hunter-gatherers who live in the Kalahari desert in Southern Africa, travelling for most of the year in bands of about thirty people. They generally divide their work according to sex, with the men doing the hunting and the women gathering plants, nuts and berries. The work of gathering involves strenuous walking and carrying and requires a detailed knowledge of the bush and of plant species. Women often help the men's hunting expeditions by passing on detailed reports of the habits and whereabouts of animals they observe during a day's gathering. The plant food which the women gather provides 60-80% of the total volume of the !Kung San's diet and is therefore a more important and more reliable food source than meat, which the men bring in from hunting on a more irregular basis. !Kung San women have a high status, and take part in group discussions and decision-making on a footing equal with men.

This photograph, taken by the anthropologist Richard Lee, shows !Kung San women gathering berries for their food. What link do you think there is between the work they do and their status in the community?

Researchers have noticed that where groups of !Kung San have been forced to settle and become farmers (rather than hunter-gatherers), the power and freedom of the women have been reduced. In this situation the men are in charge of rearing and selling livestock and trading with local people, and so the women's work of planting and harvesting is seen as less important.

ON REFLECTION:

What does research into the lives of these modern hunter-gatherers suggest about women's power in prehistoric Britain?

ANCIENT CIVILIZATIONS

Although we have little evidence of what life was like in Britain in prehistoric times, there are more clues about other parts of the world.

In Egypt, for example, there was a civilized society some 3000 years before the birth of Christ. Historians know quite a lot about this society from the large number of its tombs that have been excavated and explored. Many of these tombs contain wall-paintings depicting scenes from Egyptian life, as well as images of gods and goddesses.

Women are shown in a number of roles, from goddesses and queens to slaves, musicians, courtiers and farm labourers – which indicates that they

The tomb of Queen Hatshepsut, at the Temple of Deir El Bahari in Egypt, was photographed by the Egyptologist Edward Naville. What do you notice about Hatshepsut's appearance?

participated in every aspect of life. However, political power appears to have been held by men, who ruled as Pharoahs. There are only a few notable exceptions – for example, the queen Hatshepsut, who ruled as Pharoah for twenty years.

When Hatshepsut's tomb was discovered, the Egyptologist who deciphered the inscriptions was surprised to find that they referred to a woman:

I was still more amazed to find that all the inscriptions to do with this bearded king, attired in the familiar costume of the pharoahs, contained feminine nouns and pronouns, as though it were a matter of a queen.

(*Source:* Jean François Champollion, quoted in *Egypt of the Pharoahs*, Alan H. Gardiner, Clarendon, 1961)

Why do you suppose Hatshepsut was dressed as a man?

Why might Jean François Champollion have been so surprised at his discovery of Hatshepsut's sex?

FIRST-CENTURY BRITAIN: BOUDICA

In 61 AD, some eighteen years after the Roman invasion of Britain, the Iceni peoples of East Anglia rebelled against the Roman settlers. The Iceni, who were a wealthy tribe as far as we can tell from the remains of their pots, weapons and jewellery, were led in this revolt by a woman, Queen Boudica (sometimes called Boadicea).

Boudica's husband, the king Prasutagus, had died in 60 AD. He had named his two daughters, along with the Emperor Nero, as heirs of his estate. Roman officials, however, overlooked the daughters' inheritance and the high status of Boudica, and took all their lands from them. When Boudica resisted, she was stripped and lashed as a common criminal, and her daughters were raped. This humiliation sparked off the Iceni revolt, in which the Iceni tribe was crushed and Boudica, realizing defeat, poisoned herself.

The rebellion is recorded by two historians, the Roman Tacitus and, a century later, the Greek Dio Cassius. Both men record a speech by Boudica to her people as she led them into battle against the Romans.

Boudica's battle speech:

Boudica drove all the tribes in a chariot with her daughters in front of her. "We British are used to woman commanders in war" she cried. "I am descended from mighty men! But I am not fighting for my kingdom and wealth now. I am fighting as an ordinary person for my lost freedom, my bruised body, and my outraged daughters. . . . Consider how many of you are fighting – and why. Then you will win this battle or perish. That is what I, a woman, plan to do! – let the men die in slavery if they will."

(*Source:* Tacitus, *Annals of Imperial Rome*, translated by Michael Grant, Penguin, 1956)

"Don't fear the Romans! They protect themselves with helmets, breastplates and greaves. They provide themselves with walls and palisades and trenches. Why do they adopt such methods of fighting? Because they are afraid! . . . They can't stand hunger, thirst, cold or heat as we can. As for rivers, we swim them naked, whereas they don't get across them easily even with boats. Let us show them that they are hares and foxes trying to rule over dogs and wolves.

(*Source:* Dio Cassius, *Roman History*, translated by E. Cary, Heinemann, 1924)

Tacitus also describes the Iceni revolt in another written account:

The whole island rose under the leadership of Boudica, a lady of royal descent – for the Britons make no distinction of sex in their leaders.

(*Source:* Tacitus, *Agricola*, translated by H. Mattingly, Penguin, 1948)

What impression do these extracts give of Boudica?

What do they suggest about the position of royal women in Britain at this time?

ON REFLECTION:

How reliable do you suppose these accounts are as records both of the uprising and of what Boudica actually said (bearing their authors in mind)?

ANGLO-SAXON BRITAIN

The Romans withdrew their forces from Britain in 410 AD, by which time the social and economic order of Roman Britain was already crumbling. In 449 AD Angles, Jutes and Saxons from Northern Europe came to settle in England, and some 150 years later Christianity reached Britain.

Our knowledge of the Anglo-Saxon period comes from three main sources: written records, such as the *Anglo-Saxon Chronicle* and St Bede's *History of the English Church and People*; Anglo-Saxon poems; and artefacts excavated by archaeologists. These sources give us a number of clues about the lives of women and the extent of their power in Anglo-Saxon times.

WRITTEN RECORDS

Anglo-Saxon wills:

A number of wills exist which show noblewomen inheriting, possessing and disposing of land. A woman name Aelfgifu left 15 estates, mostly in Buckinghamshire, between the years of 966 and 975. The widow of Brihtnoth, the hero of an Anglo-Saxon poem called *The Battle of Maldon*, disposed of 36 estates and presented an elaborate tapestry depicting the heroic deeds of her husband to the monastery of Ely. The Domesday Book tells of a woman in Yorkshire named Asa who possessed land and was economically independent from her husband:

[She] . . . held her land separate and free from the domination and control of Beornwulf her husband, even when they were together so that he could neither give nor sell nor forfeit it.

(*Source:* Dorothy Whitelock, *The Beginnings of English Society*, Penguin, 1952)

The Chronicle:

The status of women of the wealthy classes appears to have been quite high. St Bede mentions Osthryth, the wife of King Oswald, as being a powerful and influential woman. *The Anglo-Saxon Chronicle* records how she was part of an assembly called to witness and sign a document from the Pope in 675 AD. The other members of the assembly were all bishops and archbishops.

Abbesses and monasteries:

Women appear to have wielded considerable power within the Christian Church at this time. Many noblewomen became Abbesses in charge of prestigious monasteries that often housed men as well as women. Bede writes at length about Hilda, a relative of King Edwin, who was Abbess first at Hartlepool, then at Whitby. She ruled over these "double" or mixed-sex monasteries, directing those under her in their studies of the Scriptures, and was a representative at an important Church council meeting at Whitby in 664 AD.

Double monasteries such as Whitby were places of distinction in learning, and it appears that women within these communities had equal access to this education. It was not only monks who undertook the painstaking and skilful work of copying Biblical texts. St Boniface asked Abbess Eadburgh to copy the Epistles of St Peter in gold script.

What does the picture suggest about the education of religious women?

In this tenth-century English manuscript St Aldhelm is shown presenting his book De Laudibus Virginitatis *to a group of nuns at Barking.*

POEMS Beowulf:

The most famous Anglo-Saxon poem is *Beowulf*, an epic tale of a noble warrior who kills the monster Grendel. In the poem we read of a warrior society of noble lords who fight, recount heroic stories of battle, and feast together in Mead Halls. Their world is male-oriented and the bond between a lord and his followers, or between male relatives, is stronger than the marriage bond.

First of all,
I went to the ring-hall to greet Hrothgar; Then there was revelry; never

in my life, under heaven's vault, have I seen men happier in the mead-hall. From time to time, the famous queen, the peace-weaver, walked across the floor, exhorting young warriors; often she gave some man a twisted gold ring before returning to her seat.

At times Hrothgar's daughter, whom I heard men call Freawaru, carried the ale-horn, offered that vessel adorned with precious metals to the thirsty warriors.

Young, and decorated with gold ornaments, she is promised to Froda's noble son . . . that match was arranged by the lord of the Scyldings, guardian of the kingdom; he believes that it is an excellent plan to use her as a peace-weaver, to bury old antagonisms, mortal feuds.

(*Source: Beowulf*, translated by Kevin Crossley-Holland, Decca, 1982)

What role are the women fulfilling in the world of the poem?

A good woman:

Another poem describes the qualities of a good queen or wife:

A woman shall prosper, be loved among her people, shall be cheerful, keep counsel, be liberal with horses and treasure; always, everywhere, greet first at the mead-drinking the protector of nobles before the band of retainers, give the first cup promptly into her lord's hand, and study the benefit of them in their housekeeping.

(*Source:* prose translation of Anglo-Saxon *Gnomic Poem* from *The Exeter Book Part II*, prose translation by Dorothy Whitelock, E.E.T.S, 1934)

How does the writer of this poem want women to behave?

ARTEFACTS

Girdle hangers such as these seem, along with keys to storerooms, cupboards and chests, to have been badges and symbols of the domestic power of women. Why might this have been?

A number of Anglo-Saxon tombs have been excavated and their contents can tell us a lot about the lives of the people buried there. It seems to have been customary for wealthy people to be buried together with their possessions. The graves of rich women contain elaborate buckles and brooches, jewellery, coins and, especially in East Anglia, large bunches of household keys and girdle hangers.

ON REFLECTION:

Look back over this chapter. Make a list of the things which empower women.

Which would a historian find most useful in building up an accurate picture of the position of women – written records, poetry, or archaeological evidence?

The Middle Ages: 1066–1500

After the Norman Conquest in the eleventh century, British society gradually became more stable, and its structures, laws and institutions were increasingly organized and regulated. Much of this new organization limited the freedom and authority of women and excluded them from exercising public power.

Despite the fact that the Middle Ages in Europe was a time of some very capable and influential queens, such as Eleanor of Aquitaine in France and Blanche of Castile in Spain, there was a tide of thought that was generally anti-women or misogynist. Educated men, following the ideas of the ancient philosopher Aristotle, believed that women were the inferior sex and so more easily influenced by evil powers. Priests and Church leaders said, on the one hand, that women were all the daughters of Eve, the original sinner, who had caused Adam to do evil. On the other hand, they praised the Virgin Mary, whose purity raised her above the normal state of womanhood. In poetry, too, women were stereotyped as either very bad or very good – as symbols of great beauty and sexuality, or bad-tempered and sharp-tongued wives.

Noah's Flood:

This is an extract from a Medieval play about Noah's flood:

NOAH: Wife, we shall be kept safe in this castle.
I wish you and my children would get in.
NOAH'S WIFE: In faith, Noah, I'd rather you slept.
For all your polite behaviour,
I shall not do what you say.
NOAH: Good wife, now do as I tell you.
NOAH'S WIFE: By Christ, not until I see more need,
Even if you stand all day and stare.
NOAH: Lord, women are always so difficult,
And never are meek, that dare I say.

(*Source:* Chester Mystery Plays *Noah's Flood*, published in *Everyman and Medieval Miracle Plays*, J.M. Dent & Sons Ltd, 1956)

What does Noah say about his wife and other women?

Women like Noah's wife are common in popular poems and tales from this period, many of which warn men about women's wickedness and instruct women how to behave decently. Since the writers were mostly men, this frequent appearance of the bossy wife in literature perhaps suggests that men were afraid of dominant women. It may also indicate that many women were discontented with the unequal distribution of power within marriages.

In the Middle Ages, when a woman married – frequently against her will and often when still in her early teens – she handed over all her land, possessions and legal rights to her husband for the duration of their marriage. Only when a woman became a widow did she regain any power or freedom in legal terms. A widow was under great pressure, from both her family and society, to marry again.

The Wife of Bath:

Geoffrey Chaucer, in his fourteenth-century poem *The Canterbury Tales*, describes a woman from Bath who has had five husbands. She says:

. . . . Marriage is a misery and a woe;
For let me say, if I may make so bold,
My lords, since when I was but twelve years old,
Thanks be to God Eternal evermore,
Five husbands have I had at the Church door!

(*Source: Wife of Bath's Prologue*, from *The Canterbury Tales*, translated by Neville Coghill, Penguin, 1951)

Why do you suppose widows were encouraged to remarry?

Look at the picture and read the following extract from *The Wife of Bath's Prologue:*

Now of my fifth husband let me tell.
God never let his soul be sent to Hell!
And yet he was my worst, and many a blow
He struck me still can ache along my row
Of ribs, and will until my dying day.

This picture showing a man beating his wife is part of woodcut made in Germany in 1456. What do the picture and the extract from the Wife of Bath's Prologue *reveal?*

Wife-beating and rape seem to have been common in the Middle Ages and were widely accepted, especially among the lower classes of society.

On the surface of things, then, it appears that women in this period had been squeezed into a position of increasing powerlessness. Yet records, documents and pictures suggest that, in reality, the extent of their influence on economic and cultural life was considerable.

HOUSEHOLDS

Despite the legal restraints placed upon wives, the domestic power of women – especially from the wealthy classes – was great. Throughout the Middle Ages, as in Anglo-Saxon times, a nobleman's wife was responsible for the management of her household. Husbands were often absent for long stretches of time, for example during the Crusades in the eleventh and twelfth centuries. Legal or political business also kept them at the Court of the King in London for long periods.

The Paston Letters:

Look at these extracts from letters exchanged by Margaret Paston and her husband in 1465. John Paston, a lawyer, spent much of his time in London, leaving Margaret to run his estate in Norfolk.

To Margaret:
I send you home writ of recovery for the sheep and the horse that were take, and advise you let the writs be delivered before my Lord of Norwich . . . and if ye make men with force to take the cattle again by warrant of recovery, spare not rather than fail.

To John:
. . . as for your wool, I may sell a stone for 40d so that I will give half year day of payment. I pray you send me word how I shall do in this matter and in all other. . .

To Margaret:
I pray you will send me hither two eln of worsted for doublets to hap me this cold winter, and that ye inquire where William Paston bought his tippet of fine worsted, which is almost like silk. And if that be finer than that, ye should buy me after 7 or 8s. . .

(*Source: The Paston Letters*, edited by Norman Davis, Oxford University Press, 1983)

Describe Margaret Paston's responsibilities.

To run a medieval middle-class household, a woman needed legal and financial knowledge, an understanding of farming, and a range of skills which included baking, brewing, spinning, weaving, fruit-growing, candle-making and, in some cases, the art of defence. Black Agnes, the Countess of Dunbar, defended her husband's castle from an attack by Edward III in 1338; this was not an uncommon event.

ON REFLECTION:

If women exercised such authority in the home, why do you suppose they were barred from public office?

WORK, TRADE AND GUILDS

Women of all classes were fully involved in working life and had considerable independence. Nevertheless, control of the economy was ultimately in male hands.

Official documents, such as poll tax registers, record urban women pursuing the following trades and crafts:

Butchers
Chandlers
Ironmongers
Netmakers
Shoemakers
Glovers
Girdlers
Haberdashers
Skinners
Retailers
Bookbinders
Silkworkers
Smiths
Spicers

An illustration taken from a fifteenth-century book entitled Le Livre des Femmes nobles et renommées *("The lives of noble and famous ladies"). What are the women in the picture doing?*

Normally, a married woman would assist in the trade or craft followed by her husband, and she would often continue the family business after his death. An unmarried woman or widow could operate a business as a "femme sole", on a more or less equal footing with men. Many wills mention girls being apprenticed to trades alongside boys. Women, particularly those of the lower classes, worked as men's equals, paying taxes and so contributing to urban prosperity.

Public recognition of this contribution was, however, largely denied to women. The craft guilds, medieval societies which protected the interests of craftsmen in a similar way to modern trade unions, seem to have excluded women from full membership, although there are records of some female participation.

Silkworkers:

The following extract is from a petition sent to King Henry VI in 1455 by a group of silkworkers who were concerned to protect their interests from foreign competition, especially from cloth-workers in the Lombardy region of Italy:

... many a worshipful woman within the city [has] lived full honourably and therewith many good households kept and many gentlewomen and others in great number like as there be more than 1000, have been drawn under them in learning the same crafts and occupation full virtuously. . .

(*Source:* Rolls of Parliament, 1455)

Silkworkers seem to have been almost exclusively women, many of whom were from the upper classes, yet there is no evidence at all of a Silkworkers' Guild. Can you suggest reasons for this?

In 1363 a statute was passed instructing a craftsman to choose one trade and confine himself to that alone. Women, on the other hand, were often engaged in more than one trade at a time.

Piers Plowman:

My wife was a weaver and woollen cloth made,
She spoke to spinsters to spin it out. . . .
I bought her barley – she brewed it to sell.
Penny ale and thick ale she poured out at one time
For labourers and lay folk that lay by themselves.
Rose the Retailer was her name;
She hath practised the retail trade for eleven winters.

(*Source:* William Langland, *The Vision of Piers Plowman*, J.M. Dent and Sons, 1978)

List the trades that occupy Rose in this passage from the fourteenth-century poem "Piers Plowman".

In this illustration for the month of June from a fourteenth-century French Book of Hours, the women in the foreground appear to be doing similar work to the men.

Perhaps women's frequent involvement in more than one trade at a time was a reason for their exclusion from the guilds.

Country life:

In rural areas, women – with the exception of rich widows – rarely exercised public power. Yet their economic contribution was great: they shared the farm labour, grew vegetables and fruit, wove cloth, cooked, laundered and bore and nursed children, who in turn shared in the household and farm labour.

MIDWIVES In the early Middle Ages, the occasion of a birth was an exclusively female event, with only women in attendance. The midwife, responsible for the safe delivery of a live child, had formidable power. This power sometimes included religious authority, since a midwife could, in emergencies, baptize a baby that was likely to die. In the absence of anaesthetics or sophisticated medical knowledge, the midwife would use herbal remedies to relieve the mother's pain, and numerous superstitious practices and old wives' tales were connected with births.

The Midwives in this picture are hastening the delivery of a baby, probably with herbal extracts. The picture is from a Medieval Herbarium *(book of plants and flowers). During the Middle Ages men became more and more involved in the birth of babies. How many reasons can you suggest for this?*

Church authorities – who became increasingly powerful in medieval society – feared the midwives and their association with magic and witchcraft. As it thought that women were morally weak and that the pain of childbirth was a woman's punishment for Eve's sin and therefore not to be removed, the Church saw the midwives' medical powers as the result of an alliance with the Devil, and believed that the death of a child during labour was caused by the midwife's evil power. The Church authorities therefore sought to control and restrict female midwifery during this period.

Church control:

The *Malleus Malificarum* of 1486, a document commissioned by the Pope to root out witchcraft, stated that all doctors must have professional training. (Since education was, by this time, confined mainly to male monasteries, this excluded the majority of women.) It said:

If a woman dare to cure without having studied . . . she is a witch and must die.

This followed a trend set in the thirteenth century by the Guild of Barbers and Surgeons, which also excluded women. The Guild granted to surgeons the sole official right to use surgical instruments, thereby ensuring that male doctors, not midwives, attended difficult births.

By 1512 midwives were required to have a Bishop's licence to operate; by 1597 they had to swear an oath promising to refrain from all sorcery and enchantment during a woman's labour.

RELIGIOUS WOMEN As the Church exerted more and more control over society and the way it was run during this period, it also tightened its own rules.

Monasteries:

Double monasteries, which had been thriving centres of education and spiritual devotion in Anglo-Saxon times, began to be closed in favour of single-sex monasteries. Conrad Marchtal, an Abbot in France, explained his reasons for excluding women from monasteries as follows:

We and our whole community of canons, recognising that the wickedness of women is greater than all the other wickednesses of the world, and that there is no anger like that of women, and that the poison of asps and dragons is more curable and less dangerous to men than the familiarity of women, have unanimously decreed for the safety of our souls, no less than for that of our bodies and goods, that we will on no account receive any more sisters . . . but will avoid them like poisonous animals.

(*Source:* E.L. Hugo, *Annales Praemonstratenses*, quoted in *Western Society and the Church in the Middle Ages*, by R.W. Southern, Penguin, 1970)

What exactly is the Abbot saying?

Whilst quality education was now for the most part confined to the male monasteries, nunneries increasingly became dumping grounds for the unmarried or unmarriageable daughters of the upper classes. They often had no desire to follow a religious life, but were placed in nunneries because there was no other respectable place in society for unmarried young women.

Mystics:

Religious life did, however, afford some women both a voice and an area of influence in a society that was becoming very male-dominated. Thomas

Aquinas, a religious thinker whose ideas had a great impact on the Church of the Middle Ages, had said that although women were incapable of Church leadership, they were able to receive the gift of prophecy (receiving spiritual messages or pictures from God). As a result of his thinking, and of the teaching of St Paul, who, in his first letter to the Corinthian Church, encouraged all believers to prophesy, it was relatively acceptable for religious or Mystic women to have and to communicate visions. Some of these women had enormous influence on the spiritual and moral life of their day. In twelfth-century Germany, the Mystic, Hildegarde of Bingen, not only wrote down her religious visions – which won her great respect – but also wrote scientific treatises, songs, plays, and a large number of influential letters to Popes, Kings and political figures of the time. These non-religious writings were taken seriously because she was exceptionally well-educated, self-confident and of high social standing.

The writings of another Mystic, Birgitta of Sweden, were widely distributed in Europe and available in England in the fourteenth century.

Birgitta of Sweden receiving her Revelations from Jesus Christ, from a Medieval manuscript entitled Revelations Celestes. *What does the picture tell us about the importance of Birgitta and her writings?*

These "Revelations" contained controversial political advice to Popes and Kings, and the French Chancellor sought to have the writings banned because of their impact.

In England, the writings of Julian of Norwich, a Mystic recluse who had a series of religious visions, were widely read and her spiritual wisdom and guidance were valued by men and women alike.

Beguines:

Mystic women who wanted to follow a devotional life without the restrictions of a normal monastic order, or who were from the lower classes and therefore not eligible to enter one of the nunneries, since these were open only to upper-class women, often lived as Beguines (pronounced *Beg-eens*). Beguine women were not members of a religious order as such, but they followed devotional lives either in informal religious communities or in families, working as nurses, seamstresses, teachers or domestic servants. They refused to have their spiritual lives directed by male leaders, and saw themselves as serving not human superiors, but Christ alone. The existence of Beguines was perhaps the result of a female reaction against male control of religious life.

The Church authorities were extremely suspicious of Beguine women, accusing them of false teaching and immoral behaviour. They tried to force them into regulated nunneries, but with mixed success. The Beguine movement had its origins in the thirteenth century in Germany and the Netherlands. Both these countries had important trade links with Norfolk and this explains why Beguine influences seem to have been strong in that part of Britain.

Margery Kempe:

One woman in Norfolk who followed a Beguine lifestyle was Margery Kempe, a brewer from King's Lynn, who gave up her prosperous business to travel the country praying, advising fellow believers and priests and receiving visions. According to her life story, *The Book of Margery Kempe*, she had considerable influence:

There was once a vicar came to this creature, asking her to pray for him and discover whether he would please God more by leaving his cure of souls and his benefice or by keeping it, because he thought he was of no use among his parishioners. The creature being in her prayers and having this matter in mind, Christ said to her spirit, "Tell the vicar to keep his cure and his benefice and be diligent in preaching and teaching to them in person, and sometimes to procure others to teach them my laws and commandments, so that there is no fault on his part, and if they don't do any better, his reward shall be none the less for it." And so she gave her message as she was commanded and the vicar still kept his cure.

(*Source: The Book of Margery Kempe*, translated by B. Windeatt, Penguin, 1985)

Margery Kempe dictated this account of her travels and spiritual experiences towards the end of her life. Written in the fourteenth century, it is the earliest known autobiography of an English person. How useful are autobiographical writings as historical evidence?

ON REFLECTION:

In which areas of life do you think women had most power in the Middle Ages?

The Sixteenth and Seventeenth Centuries

The sixteenth and seventeenth centuries saw the reigns of the Tudor and Stuart monarchs, the English Civil War, the Restoration of the monarchy, and both the Great Plague and the Fire of London. These were times of considerable upheaval and reorganization. Historical change often occurs very slowly, however, and in many ways the lives of women during these years were little different from those of their medieval forebears.

Most married women still spent a large proportion of their lives bearing and rearing children and, as in earlier centuries, many women died in childbirth. As in the Middle Ages, marriage was largely the result of family and financial arrangements – at least among the wealthy – and women still relinquished their legal rights when they married.

The Protestant Reformation improved the lot of women to a certain extent. The Puritans were opposed to wife-beating and stressed that all people, male and female, were equal in God's eyes. They also emphasized wifely obedience, however, believing that a husband was the head, or master, of his wife. It was felt that patriarchy was the natural order of things and that without this, society would break down and chaos result.

The Taming of the Shrew:

One of Shakespeare's plays is about a man teaching his bad-tempered wife to be obedient to him. This speech comes right at the end of the play and is spoken by Katherine, the wife:

Thy husband is thy lord, thy life, thy keeper,
Thy head, thy sovereign; one that cares for thee,
And for thy maintenance; commits his body
To painful labour both by sea and land,
To watch the night in storms, the day in cold,
Whilst thy liest warm at home, secure and safe;
And craves no other tribute at thy hands
But love, fair looks, and true obedience –
Too little payment for so great a debt.

(*Source:* William Shakespeare, *The Taming of the Shrew*, Act V Scene ii, *c.* 1594)

In the sixteenth and seventeenth centuries it was assumed, as it had been in the Middle Ages, that a married woman would be responsible for domestic affairs and the running of her household. Numerous books were published outlining the roles and duties of a good wife.

The Book of the Courtier:

As in previous generations, women were usually denied positions of control in the Church, politics and society. However, there was a great deal

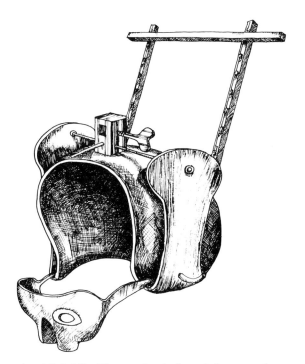

THE
ENGLISH
House-Wife,

CONTAINING

The inward and outward Vertues
which ought to be in a Compleat Woman.

As her skill *in Phyfick, Chirurgery, Cookery, Extraction of Oyls, Banqueting stuff, Ordering of great Feasts, Preferving of all fort of Wines, conceited Secrets, Distillations, Perfums,* Ordering of *Wool, Hemp, Flax :* Making *Cloath* and *Dying* ; The knowledge of *Dayries :* Office of *Malting* ; of *Oats,* their excellent ufes in Families : Of *Brewing, Baking,* and all other things belonging to an Houfhold.

A Work generally approved, and now the Ninth time much Augmented, Purged, and made moft profitable and neceffary for all men, and the general good of this NATION.

By *G. Markham.*

LONDON,
Printed for *Hannah Sawbridge,* at the Sign of the *Bible* on *Ludgate-Hill.* 1683.

A scold's bridle. Women who challenged the accepted arrangement in marriage and asserted themselves too forcefully were accused of being scolds and nags. A disobedient wife could be brought before the courts and tried as a scold. If found guilty, she was punished by being made to wear a scold's bridle on her head, or by being tied to a ducking stool and submerged in a pond.

The title page of a book by Gervase Markham. What clues does this give us about society's expectations of housewives? Does other evidence in this chapter support or contradict these clues?

of debate – especially in educated circles – about the nature and status of women, and a fashion developed for books about the balance of the sexes. One book which was popular and influential at the English Court when it was translated from Italian in 1561, was *The Book of the Courtier* by Castiglione. In the following passage, two characters are discussing women and power:

Gaspare:
I am quite surprised . . . that since you endow women with letters, continence, magnanimity and temperance you do not want them to govern cities as well, and to make laws, and lead armies, while the men stay at home and cook and spin. . .

The Magnifico:
Perhaps that would not be so bad either. Don't you think that we might find many women just as capable of governing cities and armies as men? . . .

(*Source:* B. Castiglione, *The Book of the Courtier,* translated by George Bull, Penguin, 1967)

How common do you suppose views like those of The Magnifico were?

ELIZABETH I

Elizabeth I is one example of an exceptional woman holding political power despite prevailing attitudes towards female government. Even though her birth had been greeted with disappointment because she was not a boy, she had a long and successful reign.

One man who was opposed to being ruled by a woman was John Knox, a Scottish Protestant Reformer, who published a pamphlet shortly before Elizabeth came to the throne in 1558.

The First Blast of the Trumpet Against the Monstrous Regiment of Women:

Woman in her greatest perfection was made to serve and obey man, not to rule and command him . . . a woman promoted to the seat of God, that is to teach, to judge, or to reign above man, is a monster in nature, contumely to God, and a thing most repugnant to his will.

John Knox wrote his pamphlet when there were Catholic queens on the thrones of Scotland and England (Mary Queen of Scots and Mary Tudor). Do you think the accession of Elizabeth I, a Protestant queen, to the throne of England would make him change his views?

Although much attention was drawn to Elizabeth's womanhood, and contemporary music and poetry praised her beauty and femininity, she was, like many women who succeed in traditionally male positions, inevitably seen as an exception to her sex. She reinforced this view by

This painting of Elizabeth I, known as the "Armada Portrait", was painted by the Dutch artist George Gower. What symbols of Elizabeth's power has the artist incorporated into his picture?

frequently referring to herself as a king, as in the following speech which she is alleged to have made on the eve of the arrival of the Spanish Armada on the English coast.

The Tilbury speech:

I know I have the body of a weak and feeble woman but I have the heart and stomach of a king, and of a King of England too. . .

Elizabeth's tutor, Roger Ascham, who taught her six languages, including Latin, said that her mind was "exempt from female weakness" and with a "masculine power of application".

ON REFLECTION:

From all the evidence concerning women in this period, why do you think the ability to govern and rule was frequently viewed as a male quality?

THE CIVIL WAR

Since Elizabeth's power was regarded by most as unusual and as a breach of the "natural" order (in which women were subordinate to men), her reign did little to extend or increase the power of ordinary women. Forty years after Elizabeth's death, however, the Civil War provided women with greater opportunities for experiencing freedom and authority.

Times of war and revolution tend to loosen and break down the "normal", established structures of society, and in this unsettled atmosphere women often acquire greater power than in times of stability. During the 1640s and 1650s women became relatively active and influential. They worked as nurses, spies, fund-raisers, and even as warriors and defenders. Lady Bankes defended Corfe Castle in Dorset from a siege in 1643 and was later commended for displaying "masculine" bravery and "courage above her sex". Many popular songs of the period tell stories of gallant "she-soldiers" – women who smuggled themselves into the armies in male disguise.

It was in petitioning and political protesting that women asserted themselves most forcibly, however. They found a powerful public voice several times during the 1640s:

1640 More than four hundred working-class women petitioned Parliament to protest at having been made jobless and destitute as a result of the war.

1643 Several thousand women mobbed Parliament, demanding peace and work. They were dispersed with violence and gunfire.

1647 Women working as maids petitioned Parliament, to complain about poor working conditions.

1649 Some ten thousand women, wearing the sea-green ribbons of the Levellers (a political movement with radical and democratic ideals), petitioned for the release of Leveller prisoners held in the Tower of London.

When the Leveller women's petition was rejected on the grounds that politics was not a feminine business, they presented a second petition:

Since we are assured of our creation in the image of God, of an interest in Christ equal unto men, and also of a proportionate share in the freedoms of the Commonwealth, we cannot but wonder and grieve that we should appear so despicable in your eyes as to be thought unworthy to petition or represent our grievances to this honourable House. Have we not an equal interest with the men of this nation in those liberties and securities contained in the 'Petition of Right' and other of the good laws of the land?

(*Source:* Petition, probably written by Mrs Chidley, quoted in *The Levellers and the English Revolution* by Christopher Hill, Cresset Press, 1961)

The Parliament of Women. *After the 1642 Petition, several such pamphlets written by men appeared – attacking women's involvement in politics. Many men seem to have objected to female activism because of their fear that it might result in their wives' being sexually unfaithful.*

RELIGIOUS SECTS

If some women found a political voice during the Civil War, many found freedom of expression within the "fringe" religious sects that were gathering strength in the seventeenth century. Certain groups, such as Quakers, Ranters, Shakers and Baptists, attracted large numbers of women, many of whom were illiterate and came from the lower classes of society. While the mainstream Church barred women from holding public office and prevented them from speaking, these newer groups emphasized the spiritual equality of men and women.

Women within the sects were permitted to vote, to debate, to prophesy, and sometimes to preach – since preaching was said to be the work of the "Inner Light" of Christ. George Fox, who founded the Quaker movement, wrote in 1656:

May not the Spirit of Christ speak in the female as well as in the male?

(*Source:* George Fox, *Gospel Truth*, Bodleian Library, 1656)

The power of self-expression exercised by Quaker women in the acts of preaching and prophesying was similar to the religious power of the

This satirical print shows a Quaker meeting in the seventeenth century. What was the artist's intention? Why?

Beguines and Mystic women in the Middle Ages. Female preaching was received with scorn and criticism by most of society. John Vicars, a Puritan, wrote in 1646 that it was intolerable:

> . . . to see bold impudent housewives, without all womanly modesty, to take upon them . . . to prate . . . after a narrative or discoursing manner, an hour or more. . .
>
> (*Source:* John Vicars, *The Schismatick Sifted: Or, A Picture of Independents Freshly and Fairly Washt over Again*, Bodleian Library, 1646)

Although women enjoyed some degree of power during the Civil War, and within religious communities throughout this period, the sixteenth and seventeenth centuries witnessed an increasing trend towards female powerlessness. This is particularly noticeable in the areas of economic life and education.

EDUCATION

The education of women, which was already declining in quality during the Middle Ages, suffered from the closure of the nunneries during the Protestant Reformation. This, together with the prevailing attitude that women were less intelligent than men, and that their primary function was to raise children, led to a widespread view that extensive education was not necessary for women.

In wealthy households the wife tended to teach her children and servants reading and knowledge of the Bible, but there was no formal training for this teaching role. Public education for girls was biased towards useful practical skills, such as needlework. Girls did not attend grammar schools or universities in the sixteenth and seventeenth centuries. In exceptional cases, men would give their daughters an education which included Latin and foreign languages, but generally such knowledge was reserved for boys. As in previous centuries, the lack of proper education and training excluded women from positions of power in government and such professions as medicine and law.

In 1640 a pamphlet was published defending the female sex. It was entitled *The Women's Sharpe Revenge* and its authors used the pseudonyms Mary Tattlewell and Joane Hit-him-home. On the subject of education, it said the following:

When we, whom they style by the name of weaker vessels, though of a more plyant flesh and therefore of a temper more capable of the best Impression, have not that generous and liberal education, lest we should be made able to vindicate our owne injuries, we are set only to the needle, to prick our fingers . . . we be brought up to musick, to singing, and to dancing . . . and thus if we be weak by Nature, they strive to make us more weake by our Nurture.

(*Source:* Mary Tattlewell and Joane Hit-him-home, *The Women's Sharpe Revenge*, Bodleian Library, 1640)

What link can you see between the authors' pseudonyms and the message of their pamphlet?

TRADE AND BUSINESS

In trading, crafts and city life, women – especially widows – continued to be active. Booksellers, stationers and shopkeepers, in particular, tended to be women.

By the end of the seventeenth century practically all the thread and cloth needed by Britain's booming textiles industry was produced by women. Since woven cloth constituted about one-third of British exports at this time, the female contribution to the country's economy was of major importance.

Husband and wife partnerships were still common, especially in London, and middle-class city wives seem to have enjoyed considerable freedom, independence and equality. Many plays from this period, such as Thomas Dekker's *The Shoemaker's Holiday*, contain strong-minded, economically-active female characters.

A number of changes occurred during the sixteenth and seventeenth centuries, however, and these effectively lessened women's power in industrial and commercial life. As industries such as the textile trade became more organized and more capitalist in their structure, it became more common for men to work for employers in exchange for wages, rather than simply making and selling items for themselves. This meant going out to work at an employer's premises rather than running a family business from home. Wives were then no longer involved in their husbands' trades and, as they were more tied to the home by child-rearing (and, more specifically, by breast-feeding), women were less free to seek work outside the home.

Lower-class women often took in spinning or weaving work at home, in exchange for extremely low wages, whilst the wives of more prosperous tradesmen or farmers became idle, detached from working life, and preoccupied with fashion and leisure activities. By the end of the seventeenth century female guild membership – already restricted – was dwindling and it was less and less common for a wife to be named as an executor of her husband's will.

Women lost their former control of the brewing and silk-weaving trades because of the increase in regulations favouring men and, in 1622, a proclamation restricted the practice of the lucrative gold and silk thread spinning trade to members of the Company of Gold Wire Drawers – few of whom were women.

The picture on the left is from the early sixteenth century and the picture on the right is from the end of the seventeenth century. Compare the impressions you get of the women in these two pictures. What changes do they reflect?

ON REFLECTION:

What problems are there in drawing historical conclusions from pictures?

The Eighteenth Century

With the Restoration of the Monarchy in 1660 came a renewed suppression of the claims to power made by women during the Civil War. The trend towards female powerlessness – and, among the middle classes, idleness – which began in the late seventeenth century intensified throughout the eighteenth century.

Some elements of women's lives stayed unchanged. As in previous centuries, married women were legally subject to their husbands. A wife was expected to be obedient, and economic control lay with the man.

Wife-beating:

Legal records show that, in London, wife-beating was regarded as a criminal offence as early as in the seventeenth century, but, nonetheless, this practice appears to have been widespread in the eighteenth century.

Universities and the professions continued to be closed to women in the eighteenth century, and women were not permitted to hold power, or to have a voice within the Church. Dr Johnson, who, in the 1750s, wrote one of the first dictionaries, said that the idea of a woman preaching was like that of a dog walking on his hind legs!

In the 1760s a judge decreed that it was acceptable for a man to beat his wife as long as the stick he used was no thicker than his thumb! This engraving by William Hogarth satirizes the judge's decision and is entitled "Mr Justice Thumb in the act of flagellation".

AGRICULTURE AND INDUSTRY

During this century there were major changes in agriculture and industry. As a result of better farming techniques, which led to increased agricultural production, the country grew more prosperous. At the same time, there was a significant increase in the size of the population, partly as a result of an improved diet. These changes, however, helped to contribute to the growing position of powerlessness of many women.

England in the eighteenth century still had a mainly agrarian or farming economy. At the beginning of the century, agriculture involved the majority of the population and their livelihood depended on a good harvest. Within farming households, wives performed an important role, supervising dairying and cheesemaking. Women often worked at ploughing, harrowing and driving carts, and frequently girls were apprenticed to farm work. If a harvest was bad, poorer women undertook work such as spinning, and producing thread and cloth at home, in exchange for low wages. In this way, wives often saved their families from starvation and therefore their power as providers was immense, giving them prestige within households and communities.

According to letters published in the *Annals of Agriculture*, a farming journal, women were involved in the developments and improvements in farming techniques. For example, Mrs Coke of Fishponds, near Bristol, was noted for cultivating a new crop, chicory, to feed to her pigs. Many women are listed as prizewinners at livestock shows.

Wealthy wives:

Improvements in farming reduced the economic power of women, however. New techniques increased the size of harvests, and as larger farms grew more wealthy, farmers appointed farm managers and servants to do the work previously done by their wives. In many country towns, markets where women had once sold their dairy produce and poultry virtually died out during this period.

Products such as soap, beer and starch, which had formerly been made at home, were increasingly bought from shops, so that running a household became simpler and less demanding. As consumers rather than producers, the wives of prosperous farmers became idle and sought to imitate the upper classes in their leisured lifestyles. Many of them could now afford to dress, eat and behave like upper-class women, and this improved their social status. At the same time it undermimed their real power, since economically, they became dependants rather than contributors.

Poor farmers:

Many small farming families were driven off the land by changes in agriculture. Either their land was swallowed up by more prosperous farmers who were expanding their farms and increasing the size of their fields, or they were unable to afford new machinery, and so became uncompetitive. They were forced either to work as seasonal farm labourers on someone else's land, or to move to the newly industrialized towns and seek work there.

Sessions papers:

Sessions papers or Court records show the occupations of the witnesses, prisoners and prosecutors appearing at the Old Bailey.

Date	Man	Wife
Sept 1737	Sells milk	Hawks fruit
April 1745	Driver to a hackney coachman	Takes in washing
May 1748	Sailor (alleged)	Shoplifter; says she "works at her needle"
Jan 1759	Recruiting sergeant in the guards	Sells old clothes, used to keep a public house
Oct 1759	Shoe-maker	Deals in old iron and rags, "keeps a broker's shop"
Dec 1766	Chairman	Keeps "house of lodgers" and sells pease porridge and sheep's heads in her shop
April 1781	Tailor	Mantua-maker, takes in lodgers
July 1783	"A lame man who cannot earn his bread"	Keeps a greens shop
Sept 1788	Watchman	Sells cakes and gingerbread
Sept 1788	Saloop seller (helps wife)	Saloop seller in Moorfields
Sept 1789	Labourer	Makes up children's frocks and bed gowns
Sept 1789	Watchman	Quilter
Sept 1794	Porter	Takes in washing, formerly had a milk-walk

What do these records show about married women's occupations in London?

Industrialization greatly changed the lives of women in the poorer classes. The mechanization of many trades, which meant that fewer people were needed to do the same amount of work, coupled with an increase in the population, created a surplus of labour which led to competition for jobs, and therefore employers were able to offer very low wages. Women's wages were lower than men's since it was thought that higher wages would tempt women away from their domestic duties (housekeeping and child-rearing) into industry. Women for whom factory work was a financial necessity were therefore regarded as cheap labour, and were exploited in appalling conditions.

Book of Prices:

Piece-work regulations often restricted the amount of work that women could do. In 1769 *A List of Prices*, agreed to by masters and men in the weaving trade, laid out the following conditions:

No woman or girl to be employed in making any kind of work except such works as are herein fixed and settled at 5½d. per ell or . . . per yard or under for the making and those not to exceed half an ell in width. . . . And no woman or girl is to be employed in making any sort of handkerchief of above the usual or settled price of 4s. 6d. per dozen for the making thereof PROVIDED always . . . that in case it shall hereafter happen that the Kingdom of Great Britain shall engage in war . . . that then every manufacturer shall be at liberty to employ women or girls in the making of any sort of works as they shall think most fit and convenient without any restraint whatsoever. . .

(*Source: A List of Prices*, 1769, Goldsmiths Library)

How and why is women's work being restricted?

The separation of home and workplace created by factories meant that for many women their traditional domestic power and matriarchal influence were reduced. The home was no longer a focus of economic life, and work outside the home meant that mothers were separated from their children or had to take them into the factories, where the health risks were considerable. On the other hand, being a wage earner meant an improvement in status, especially for unmarried women, as it freed them from dependence on male relatives.

THE FEMININE IDEAL

As women of the wealthier classes began to lose their usefulness in society, their lives became dominated by leisure and fashion. Girls were brought up to be Ladies, the ideal lady being virtuous, beautiful, polite, sexually passive, and always "correct" in her social behaviour.

Magazines such as this one, printed in 1761, contained songs, essays and theatre reports, as well as love-letters and society gossip. How do the cover and contents differ from those of a women's magazine of today?

This feminine ideal was reinforced by the popular literature of the period. Magazines such as *The Female Tatler* and *The Lady's Magazine* became popular with upper-class ladies.

Reading novels was a favourite female pursuit in the eighteenth century. One bestseller was *Pamela* by Samuel Richardson, which tells the story of a virtuous and innocent servant girl who fends off the sexual advances of her master and finally transforms his behaviour by her goodness. In the end she is rewarded by marrying him, which she regards as the highest honour since he is her social superior. Pamela typifies the eighteenth-century ideal of womanhood, in that she is angelic, passive, charming and innocent.

Mary Wollstonecraft:

Mary Wollstonecraft was a writer who rejected the notion of the feminine ideal. She challenged the patriarchal organization of British society and the idea that power was a male preserve, having herself struggled tobecome financially independent. Despite her meagre education, she became a journalist and teacher after having worked for a time in what were thought of as more suitably feminine jobs, as a lady's companion and then as a governess. She is often thought of as the mother of the modern feminist movement. Her best-known book, *Vindication of the Rights of Women*, was written in 1792. In it she attacks the contemporary view of marriage and wifeliness, the female preoccupation with fashion and leisure, and the state of women's education. Her ideas had the support of a number of contemporary writers, thinkers and Radicals – most of them men – with whom she was friendly.

This picture of Mrs Congreve and her family was painted in 1782 by the English artist Philip Reinagle. The Congreves were relatives of the eighteenth-century playwright William Congreve. Family group portraits of this type were very popular in the eighteenth century.

ROMANCE AND MARRIAGE

In the eighteenth century, marriage among the upper classes and gentry was based more and more on romantic love rather than on economic convenience. The idea of "falling in love" and the rituals of courtship dominated fiction. In the novels of Jane Austen, a marriage based on genuine love is seen as the ultimate fulfilment of a woman's purpose. Family life was viewed as an important factor in maintaining a stable and well-ordered society.

Mary Wollstonecraft objected to the imbalance in marriages of the time, where the only power a woman possessed lay in her ability to charm and manipulate a doting husband. By being the object of his adoration and passion, and by seeking always to please him, a wife could have her husband "in her power".

FASHION AND ADORNMENT

Since an attractive and well-dressed wife was a social asset to her husband, and since the ideal wife aimed to please, a great deal of women's energy was spent on fashion and adornment. Mary Wollstonecraft criticized the attention to appearance which she witnessed in Lady Kingsborough's household, where she was governess for a time:

> You cannot conceive the dissipated lives the women of quality lead. Five hours do many, I assure you, spend in dressing – without making preparations for bed, washing with Milk of Roses etc. etc. . . . .

(*Source:* Mary Wollstonecraft, letter to her sister quoted in *William Godwin*, by C. Kegan Paul, London, 1876)

EDUCATION

The education of upper- and middle-class girls was geared towards leisure and wifeliness, and served to reinforce the accepted feminine ideal. Schools such as Sloane House taught girls such accomplishments as music, dancing and playing cards, so that they could provide entertainment for their business-minded husbands. Subjects like botany and biology were not taught because they were considered improper, and history, philosophy and Classical languages were thought to be too rigorous for

This trade card advertising a London girls' school was printed in 1797. Describe the education being offered by Sloane House School.

female minds. Young girls spent a great deal of time confined indoors, occupied with needlework or playing stringed instruments, and so they lacked fresh air and exercise. This resulted in their being physically frail. Novels of the period are full of tales of delicate women catching colds from getting wet and fainting from over-excitement. Mary Wollstonecraft saw this kind of education as a major cause of women's powerlessness. She proposed that girls should be given the same education as boys. In her *Vindication* she wrote:

Women have been allowed to remain in ignorance and slavish dependence many, very many years, and still we hear nothing but their fondness of pleasure and sway, their childish attachment to toys, their preference for rakes and soldiers, and the vanity that makes them value accomplishments more than virtues.

(*Source:* Mary Wollstonecraft, *A Vindication of the Rights of Women*, Penguin, 1985)

An anonymous pamphlet entitled *Sophia* was published in 1737. It made a connection between women's lack of education and their lack of public power. It asked:

Why is learning useless to us? . . . Because we have no share in public offices, and why have we no share in public offices? Because we have no learning.

(*Source: Sophia*, Bodleian Library, 1737)

It was because they recognized the connection between knowledge and power that many members of the ruling class in the eighteenth century opposed and feared educating the poorer classes. What little education there was available for them – provided by charity schools – aimed to teach obedience and hard work. It concentrated on drill work to foster discipline and submission.

Radical ideas like those of Mary Wollstonecraft gained some ground during the 1790s, when the French Revolution created ripples of nonconformism and free thought in Britain. However, this challenge to patriarchal power structures was an isolated pocket of influence, just as the upsurgence of radical ideas in the English Civil War had been. By the end of the century the ideas of the conservative philosopher Rousseau were more dominant. He saw women as child-bearing and domestic and, indeed, as overgrown children themselves.

ON REFLECTION:

From the evidence in this chapter how widespread do you think the idea of the feminine ideal was in the eighteenth century?

The Nineteenth Century

Historians know a great deal more about the lives of Victorian women than about those in earlier centuries, as many more records exist. Society was more widely literate, and so there is ample written material – newspapers, letters, diaries, books and novels. There are also houses, clothes, and objects, and there are taped recordings of people recalling the years of the nineteenth century stored in archives. During the nineteenth century Britain continued to change from a rural to an industrialized and urbanized society.

In 1870 Queen Victoria publicly denounced a lecture which had been given on "The Claims of Women". This lecture, given by Lady Amberley, put forward views on women's rights which the Queen found unacceptable. What does her message show about her attitude to women's power?

The Queen is most anxious to enlist everyone to join in checking this mad, wicked folly of Women's Rights, with all its attendant horrors.... Woman would become the most hateful, heartless and disgusting of human beings were she allowed to unsex herself; and where would be the protection which man was intended to give the weaker sex?

Queen Victoria

As society changed, it became more complex and people's lifestyles and circumstances became more varied. In terms of power, women's experiences were very mixed. Despite there being a woman on the English throne for most of the century, there was still much opposition to the idea of women exercising public authority.

Amongst the increasing numbers of the middle class, the accepted feminine ideal continued to shape the expectations placed on women. As prosperity increased, families spent more money on home furnishings, furniture and household goods. As homes became more sumptuous and upholstered, and women's fashions became more bulky and restricting, the idea of the fragile, protected, domestic and "womanly" female gathered momentum.

The Angel of the House:

The novelist Virginia Woolf grew up in the nineteenth century. When she began to write in the early twentieth century, she was haunted by the image of Victorian womanhood and its impact on her generation.

> You who come of a younger and happier generation may not have heard of the Angel of the House. She was intensely sympathetic. She was immensely charming. She was utterly unselfish. . . . Almost every Victorian house had its angel. And when I came to write, the shadow of her wings fell upon the page; I heard the rustling of her skirts in the room.
>
> (*Source:* Virginia Woolf, "A Speech to Professional Women", given in 1931 and published in *The Pargiters*, Hogarth Press, 1978)

A Manchester woman:

In her autobiography one middle-class woman, Katherine Chorley, describes life in a suburb of Manchester in the late nineteenth century. While standing on a station platform, she tried to sketch people's faces:

> I could not sketch the ladies on the same plane as their husbands and fathers and sons because it would not come natural to put them on an equality. For the men were the money-lords; and since for almost every family the community values were fundamentally economic, it followed that their women were their dependants. They existed for their husbands' and fathers' sakes and their lives were shaped to please masculine vanity.
>
> (*Source:* K. Chorley, *Manchester Made Them*, Faber & Faber, 1950)

What do these two extracts reveal about Victorian attitudes to the sexes?

FEMINIST REFORM Although the image of women as passive, powerless and angelic pervaded nineteenth-century society, there is evidence that many women rejected the constraints placed on them by the feminine ideal.

Florence Nightingale:

Look at this extract from the diary of Florence Nightingale, written in 1846 before she began nursing:

> What is my business in this world and what have I done in the last fortnight? I have read *The Daughter at Home* to Father and two chapters of Mackintosh; a volume of *Sybil* to Mama. Learnt seven tunes by heart. Written various letters. Ridden with Papa. Paid eight visits. Done company. And that is all.
>
> (*Source:* *The Diary of Florence Nightingale*, 7 July 1846, edited by E. Cook, Macmillan, 1913)

Florence Nightingale's discontent with the life of idleness that was the lot of many middle-class women appears to have been typical. Numerous Victorian middle-class women poured their energies into charitable acts as an outlet for their longing to do practical work. Philanthropy, or the doing of good works, was seen as a suitable female occupation, since it was concerned with caring. Women visited the poor and sick or joined Girls' Friendly Societies which organized charitable projects. They were involved with administering workhouses and charity schools and were at the forefront of campaigns for the abolition of slavery, for Temperance, and for women's suffrage (the right to vote).

Many of the women who devoted themselves to improving society were motivated by their radical Christian faith. They believed in the spiritual equality of the sexes and rejected the traditional restraints placed on women by the Church:

- Mary Carpenter set up orphanages and reform schools in Bristol.
- Annie Besant supported the match girls in their strike for better pay and campaigned for greater availability of birth control.
- Octavia Hill organized Housing Reform.
- Florence Nightingale made huge advancements in nursing and public health.
- Josephine Butler campaigned for the repeal of the Contagious Diseases Act which victimized female prostitutes.

As women such as these became involved in public life, and as the feminist movement gathered momentum, more people began to challenge both the accepted structures of patriarchy and the Victorian stereotype of womanhood.

EDUCATION One of the major goals of Victorian feminists was to achieve equal schooling for both sexes. Like Mary Wollstonecraft a century before, they believed that educational reform was a key issue of women's power. By the middle of the nineteenth century, education at primary level was widely available for boys and girls, as the 1833 Factory Act had made it compulsory for factory owners to provide elementary education for their child workers. There was, however, a total lack of secondary schooling or higher education for women. This absence of academic training kept women out of the professions, and therefore out of positions of public leadership, just as in previous generations. As a result of pressure from educational reformers, a number of significant changes occurred in the nineteenth century.

Secondary schools:

Two important girls' Secondary schools were established during the nineteenth century: the North London Collegiate School for Ladies was founded in 1837 by Frances Buss, and Cheltenham Ladies' College was founded by Dorothea Beale in 1858. The daughters of the middle classes who attended these schools had lessons in the mornings but continued to spend the afternoons at home, fulfilling their domestic duties. Their brothers, by contrast, were sent away to Public Schools, where their learning could be uninterrupted.

Many people feared the effect that serious education would have on girls. Some male gynaecologists and educationalists believed that strenuous academic study would interrupt girls' menstrual flow, thus making them infertile. There were also grave doubts about female intellectual capacities. An all-male Royal Commission which was set up in 1864 to investigate the state of education in Public Schools asked the question: "Are girls capable of learning subjects like Latin and Mathematics?"

This cartoon, drawn by "an Amateur" in 1809, caricatures girls' education. What do you think the artist intended to show?

The aim of education:

Many women opposed further education for girls:

The aim of education is to fit children for the position of life which they are hereafter to occupy. Boys are to be sent out into the world, to buffet with its temptations, to mingle with bad and good, to govern and direct. The school is the type of life they are hereafter to lead. Girls are to dwell in quiet homes, amongst a few friends; to exercise a noiseless influence, to be submissive and retiring. There is no connexion between the bustling mill-wheel life of a large school and that for which they are supposed to be preparing.

(*Source:* Elizabeth Sewell, *Principles of Education*, Bodleian Library, 1865)

Compare Elizabeth Sewell's view of women's education with that of Mary Wollstonecraft in the previous chapter (page 34). Which view do you think was most prevalent in the nineteenth century?

Universities:

Some London colleges admitted women in the 1830s and 1840s.

Cambridge admitted women in 1871 and Oxford in 1879, although women were not awarded Degrees from Oxford until after the First World War nor from Cambridge until 1949. In the 1890s Ellen Watson outdid her male contemporaries by gaining the highest marks in her year for Maths and Mechanics at University College, London.

The Society for the Employment of Women set up vocational training centres for women, such as this typewriting office in London.

Employment:

Nursing, teaching and librarianship were increasingly viewed as "respectable" occupations for ladies, as were clerical and secretarial jobs.

Most of these improvements in education directly affected only middle-class girls. What impact do you suppose they had on society as a whole?

As the number of educated women grew and women became increasingly active in public life, there was considerable pressure for them to be recognized as equal to men in other ways.

MARRIAGE AND DOMESTIC LIFE

As a result of this pressure, marriage and property laws underwent radical changes in the 1880s and 1890s. The changes gave women:
— the right to divorce
— the right to have custody of their children
— the right to inherit from a husband
— the right to own and to transfer property
— the right to have a personal savings account

Which of these changes do you think would have the most impact on women's lives?

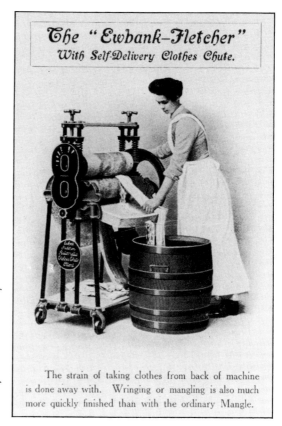

The "Ewbank-Fletcher"
With Self-Delivery Clothes Chute.

The strain of taking clothes from back of machine is done away with. Wringing or mangling is also much more quickly finished than with the ordinary Mangle.

Nineteenth-century technological improvements changed the lifestyles of many women. Plumbing, bath tubs, vacuum cleaners, sewing machines, improved stoves and new washing machines like this "Ewbank Fletcher" model reduced the burden of housework for those who could afford them.

Domestic life in the nineteenth century changed not only as a result of legal reforms but as a consequence of technological advancements, and new ideas about motherhood, childbirth and contraception.

Motherhood:

Improved medical technology and especially new ideas about child psychology changed society's view of children and the nature of motherhood. In pre-industrial society, family life had been built around economics — parenthood was about providing for the material needs of your children. In this context the father, as the family's main economic provider, generally supervised the care and training of the children. Now, as the emotional needs of children were better recognized and understood, the importance of the mother-figure was highlighted. The mother became responsible for the children's development, both physical and emotional, and was expected to entertain and educate them as well as to sustain them materially. Child-care manuals, such as *The Wife's Handbook* by Dr Allbutt, became popular and widely read.

Can you think of any disadvantages of viewing motherhood so highly?

Childbirth:

For some women, medical improvements and a better understanding of

This picture, entitled "Admiring the Newcomer", was printed in Echoes *magazine in 1869.* Echoes *was a weekly publication which aimed to represent the taste of its day and echo popular feeling.*

the body's functioning during pregnancy and birth gave them greater control over their childbearing. The increased availability of written information meant that more women knew about the importance of adequate rest and a good diet during pregnancy and about the necessity of hygienic conditions for birth. Consequently, they were more likely to demand adequate pre- and post-natal supervision and better standards of hygiene in maternity care. As a result, far fewer women now died in childbirth.

Moreover, as the use of anaesthetics during labour was introduced in the second half of the nineteenth century, women were able to exercise some control over the pain of childbirth, which the Church had said for centuries was the female's punishment for Eve's sin.

Contraception:

Even more significantly, women began to gain control over their fertility. The development of contraceptive devices allowed women the freedom to space and regulate their pregnancies and to limit the number of children they chose to have. It is impossible for historians to estimate accurately how widely family planning was used, but methods such as sponges, douches and diaphragms certainly became available in the early decades of the nineteenth century. The increased availability of birth control met with great resistance, however. In 1877 Annie Besant and Charles Bradlaugh were arrested and brought to trial for publishing and distributing Knowlton's *Fruits of Philosophy*, a book that described birth control techniques.

Working-class women:

It is probable that the increased domestic power that resulted from the new concept of motherhood, the development of household appliances, and wider knowledge of birth control and pregnancy affected only the middle classes. It is very unlikely that working-class women, with little education, and whose time and energy were spent on feeding and clothing their families, were greatly touched by these developments. However, despite being relatively unaffected by the increases in power that were changing the lives of the middle classes, women of the working class were experiencing power of a different kind. Although their lives were often characterized by immense hardship and physical toil, poorer women did not suffer the powerlessness associated with idleness and economic dependence. In many ways, they experienced greater independence and self-determination than middle-class women.

Working-class women generally made a more equal contribution to their households than their middle-class sisters, and although there was still a general division of labour – men were providers, women were housewives – the division between home and workplace was less complete than in middle-class families. Many poorer women supplemented their income by taking in other people's laundry and ironing, or by housing lodgers. (In the late nineteenth century it is estimated that one-third of all working-class women took in lodgers.) Consequently, even wives who were not in paid employment were not insulated from economic life in the way that wealthier women were.

Look at this extract in which a Victorian woman describes her mother:

As our family increased and my father's wages remained stationary, it was necessary for my mother to earn money to help keep us in food and clothing. . . . A good father and husband up to a point he [Mrs Smith's father] left responsibility of the whole family to my mother . . . the worry of all her liabilities and the continual grinding away at work for her own family and working outside her home at last undermined her once splendid constitution. . . . My mother was everything to me. I always thought whatever she did or said was sure to be right.

(*Source:* Mrs F.H. Smith, *In a Mining Village,* from *Life as We Have Known It,* by Co-operative Working Women, edited by Margaret Llewelyn Davies, Virago, 1977)

How much power does the woman described here have?

WORK AND TRADE UNIONS

In 1841, 50% of all female workers in factories were under 20 years of age. Factory workers often worked long hours in intense heat, poor light and poorly ventilated buildings where protection from dangerous equipment was inadequate. Female workers frequently suffered sexual assault by male foremen. As in the eighteenth century, their wages were poor, and lower than those of their male colleagues.

From 1824, when trade unions became legal, many working women joined unions to campaign not only for reduced hours, better conditions and better pay, but also for wider political reforms. In 1874 Emma Paterson formed the Women's Protective and Provident League to encourage the formation and growth of women's trade unions. This league was particularly necessary since there was, predictably, widespread opposition to feminine political activity.

Compare the following speech made to the Female Political Union of Newcastle upon Tyne in 1839 with Mrs Chidley's Civil War Petition on pages 23-24. What do they have in common?

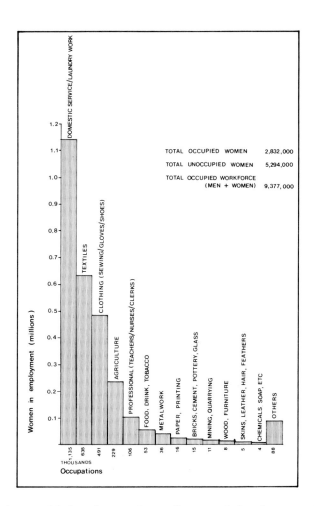

TOTAL OCCUPIED WOMEN 2,832,000

TOTAL UNOCCUPIED WOMEN 5,294,000

TOTAL OCCUPIED WORKFORCE
(MEN + WOMEN) 9,377,000

This graph shows the pattern of women's work at the time of the 1851 census. What conclusions can be drawn from these statistics?

We have been told that the province of woman is her home and that the field of politics should be left to men; this we deny; the nature of things renders it impossible, and the conduct of those who give the advice is at variance with the principles they assert. Is it not true that the interests of our Fathers, husbands and brothers ought to be ours? If they are oppressed and impoverished do we not share those evils with them? If so, ought we not to resent the infliction of those wrongs upon them?

(*Source:* quoted in Dorothy Thompson, *The Early Chartists*, London, 1971)

Opposition to female union membership also came from male trade unionists. For two reasons, they favoured an arrangement where men worked and women stayed at home. Firstly, they were likely to get better wages if they could argue that a man's wage had a whole household dependent upon it. Secondly, in situations where the population was large and work was scarce, men saw female workers as creating unnecessary competition in the labour market. Neither of these reasons takes unmarried women into account, however. In the 1840s, it was estimated that for every 1000 men there were 1050 women. This was the result of war, emigration, and higher infant mortality in boys. Thus, for many women, dependence on a male "bread-winner" was not an available option. So-called "surplus" women were a problem in Victorian Britain.

This Victorian cartoon satirizes the attitudes of employers such as Bryant & May. How much power do you think the match-girls had?

The match-girls' strike:

In 1888 Annie Besant published in the Socialist League paper details both of the dividends of shareholders of the Bryant & May Match Company and, by contrast, of the low wages of the company's female workers, many of whom worked eleven- or twelve-hour days. The managers of the company insisted that the girl employees sign a document denying Annie Besant's information. The match-girls refused to sign:

In vain he [the foreman] threatened and scolded; the girls would not sign. . . . A girl pitched on apparently as the ring-leader was threatened with dismissal, but stood firm. On the following morning she was suddenly discharged on a pretended act of insubordination, and the women, promptly seeing the reason for her punishment, put down their work with one accord and marched out. . . . The news spread, and the rest of the wood-match girls followed their example, some 1,400 women suddenly united in a common cause.

(*Source: Link*, 14 July 1888)

Annie Besant and her colleagues organized a strike fund and persuaded the London Trades Council to intervene and negotiate with the directors of Bryant & May. The match-girls won their case within a fortnight.

In the 1880s there were a number of other strikes amongst women workers – notably blanket-weavers, cigar-makers and tin-box factory girls. Working-class women realized that their labour was their power: by going on strike, and withdrawing the economic contribution they had made for generations, they could influence the decision-makers, who wielded power of a more official kind.

ON REFLECTION:

What do you think were the most important changes affecting women's power in the nineteenth century? Make a list of them.

The Twentieth Century

The twentieth century has witnessed more rapid and more significant changes than any previous era. Huge advancements in science and technology, medicine, transport, space exploration and industry have changed everyday life and given the human race a greater sense of power than ever before. Two World Wars and the development of nuclear weapons have demonstrated the immense potential human beings have to destroy each other. They have also stirred in many people the desire to use power positively, to achieve peace, justice and freedom.

In this century women have held and exercised more power than in previous generations. They have become company directors, civil servants, politicians and leaders of trade unions.

WARTIME BRITAIN

During the years that Britain was at war, women were given access to jobs and responsibilities previously denied them.

The First World War:

Between 1914 and 1918 it is estimated that nearly 800,000 women entered British industry. Although women took on men's jobs, they were paid lower wages and were not permitted to join men's trade unions.

After the war they were expected to relinquish their jobs. An article in the *Daily Graphic* said:

The idea that because the State called for women to help the nation, the

This photograph of women tarring roads was taken during the First World War.

A WAAC poster. During the war years, women were expected to take the place of men.

State must continue to employ them is too absurd for serious women to entertain.

(*Source:* quoted in David Mitchell, *Women on the Warpath*, London, 1966)

By 1921 the number of women in the British workforce was the same as in 1911. These figures indicate that the vast majority of women who took up jobs during the war had relinquished them within three years of the war's end.

The Second World War:

In the Second World War, as in the First, women were expected to replace men. In some factories during the war years women made up 80% of the workforce. Some 90,000 women enrolled for agricultural work with the Women's Land Army. Women working fewer than 55 hours per week were expected to enrol as firewatchers, and the Women's Royal Voluntary Service (WRVS), made up mostly of middle-class women, organized house clearing and distribution of relief supplies to bombed-out families.

ON REFLECTION:

What similarities are there between women's roles in the First and Second World Wars and in the English Civil War?

Why do times of war afford women greater power?

CHILDCARE AND BIRTH CONTROL

After 1945 women retained positions of responsibility far more than they had after the First World War, despite a backlash of opinion in the 1950s that women should stay at home rather than follow paid employment. The substantial changes brought to women's work by the Second World War have been reinforced by developments in birth control and childcare. In 1914 Sylvia Pankhurst started a crèche for the children of female factory workers, to enable women to work without jeopardizing their children's health and safety. During the Second World War the government provided nursery places for some 72,000 children in order to free their mothers to take up jobs. The increased availability of crèches, nurseries and childminding facilities in the twentieth century has allowed more women to work and to exercise public power.

Even more significant, however, have been this century's advancements in birth control. The first birth control clinic was opened in 1921 by Marie Stopes, who three years earlier had published a book called *Married Love*, which described methods of contraception. Increased availability of contraceptives and the development in the 1950s of the Pill have given women important control over their fertility, enabling them to be more active in public and professional life.

Why is birth control an important issue in women's power?

Women have always made a major contribution to the economic life of Britain, but in the twentieth century they have, for the first time, gained political control and representation.

SUFFRAGE The battle for votes for women first gained momentum in the 1860s, when John Stuart Mill presented a petition signed by women to Parliament. Suffrage, or the right to vote, was an important issue for women not only because it would at last give them some access to law and decision-making, but also because it represented public acknowledgment of their equality with men. During the nineteenth century the women supporters, or suffragists, campaigned for the vote by peaceful and legal means, but by the end of the 1890s their cause had dwindled.

In 1903 Emmeline Pankhurst formed the Women's Social and Political Union (WSPU). Frustrated by lack of both public and Parliamentary attention to their cause and by their powerlessness, the members of this union, or suffragettes, began to use more troublesome methods. As well as organizing marches and rallies, they defaced buildings, broke windows and destroyed letter boxes. Later, they set fire to buildings and in 1913 one suffragette, Emily Davison, died when she threw herself in front of the King's horse at the Derby.

Votes for Women:

The suffragettes used a wide range of media to publicize their cause. This is an extract from a play called *Votes for Women*, written in 1907 by Elizabeth Robins. In this scene a working woman is addressing a crowd in Trafalgar Square:

Some of you know wot the 'omes is like where the men don't let the women manage. Well . . . the 'ole government is just in the same muddle because the men 'ave tried to do the national 'ousekeeping without the women.

Roars.

But, like I told you before, it's a libel to say it's only the well-off women wot's wanting the vote. Wot about the 96,000 textile workers? Wot about the Yorkshire tailoresses? I can tell you wot plenty o' the poor women think about it. I'm one of them, and I can tell you we see there's reforms needed. *We ought to 'ave the vote (jeers)* and we know 'ow to appreciate the other women 'oo go to prison fur tryin' to get it fur us!

(*Source:* Elizabeth Robins, "Votes for Women" from *How the Vote Was Won*, a collection of suffragette plays, edited by Dale Spender and Carole Hayman, Methuen, 1985)

Suffrage was not just a middle-class cause. Many of its most active supporters were working-class women, a large number of whom were from northern industrial towns, where they formed their own Suffrage Societies. When the WSPU organized a suffragette march in London on the occasion of the Coronation of George V in 1911, 40,000 women turned out, having travelled by train from all over Britain.

This picture shows the Clitheroe Women's Suffrage Society on Nelson station on their way to the march held on the coronation of King George V.

The vote for women was won in 1918. Although the suffragettes were not directly responsible for this change, their movement had served to draw attention to women's desire for power.

WOMEN IN PARLIAMENT

Once women had won the right to representation in Parliament, a Bill was immediately passed allowing them to stand as Members of Parliament. In the 1918 General Election a suffragette, Countess Markiewicz, was elected, but her election was invalidated because she refused to swear an oath of loyalty to the King. In the following year Nancy Astor became the first woman MP.

David Lloyd-George, who was Prime Minister when Nancy Astor was elected, felt that women had an important contribution to make to the "National Government" as his coalition was called:

Now that women have been enfranchised I think it important there should be a certain number of women in Parliament. . . . There are a good many questions in regard to housing, child welfare, food, drink, and prices in which it would be an immense advantage . . . to have a woman's view presented by a woman.

(*Source:* quoted in Anthony Masters, *Nancy Astor, a Life*, Weidenfeld & Nicolson, London, 1981)

To which areas of public life did Lloyd-George think women would contribute?

Compare his speech with that of the woman in "Votes for Women".

Two Acts which were passed soon after women were enfranchised reflected a growing awareness in Parliament of women's issues. The Maternity and Child Welfare Act of 1918 established women's health clinics, and the 1919 Sex Disqualification Act ruled that women could no longer be barred from the professions because of sex or marriage.

The later decades of this century saw little further legislation for sexual equality, however, and not until the 1970s were any significant Acts passed by Parliament. In 1970 the Equal Pay Act granted women the same pay as men for doing similar jobs, and in 1975 the Sex Discrimination Act made it illegal to discriminate on grounds of sex in employment and training, education, housing, and the provision of goods, services, or facilities.

Despite the fact that women have the vote and the right to enter Parliament, it is still regarded as exceptional for a woman to rise to prominence in public life. Since 1918 there have been only three female Cabinet Ministers. The following table was compiled in 1984 by the 300 Group, an organization formed to get more women into Parliament:

Country	% women MPs	Country	% women MPs
Britain	3.6	Italy	7.9
Australia	4.8	W. Germany	9.8
USA	4.8	Switzerland	11.0
France	5.7	China	21.2
India	6.3	Sweden	28.0
Israel	6.7	Russia	32.5

(*Source: 300 Group News*, 1984)

Can you suggest reasons for the low proportion of women MPs in Britain?

The woman MP also suffers a good deal of difficulty and criticism by virtue of her gender. There are practical problems, such as the shortage of lavatories, and the lack of changing facilities, which can hamper efficiency in the new MP and in the minister. . . . Apart from poor physical facilities, the woman MP or minister is excluded from much of the informal colleagueship of what is essentially a male club, and is thus barred from much of what happens. Then she is likely to face a barrage of criticism, for if she is married she is neglecting her family, if single she is out of touch with family life. If she campaigns on feminist issues she is accused of neglecting her constituents and trivialising politics; if she does not, then she is neglecting to serve the women of the country. Her clothes, speech, hair style and behaviour are subject to constant appraisal, and her private life has to be beyond reproach. In short, the woman in the political elite suffers all the disadvantages of any professional woman, with none of the compensations of power and authority which might soften the hardship.

(*Source:* Sara Delamont, *The Sociology of Women*, Allen & Unwin, 1980)

MARGARET THATCHER

In the light of the low proportion of women in Parliament, the rise of Margaret Thatcher to be first leader of the Conservative Party in 1975 and then Prime Minister in 1979 is remarkable. Popular cartoons frequently portray Mrs Thatcher as a man. She has been both admired and attacked for her so-called "masculine" style of leadership. When she became Party leader, one Labour MP commented that she was the "best man" for the job. Her route to power followed a course traditionally that of male politicians – a grammar school and Oxford education, a spell in industry, and then entry into the legal profession. Her career strategy was interrupted only briefly by childbearing and motherhood – she has twins, who were looked after by a nanny when they were small.

Feminists have criticized Margaret Thatcher for failing to promote women's interests and for surrounding herself with male Ministers. She, however, sees herself as representing women:

> The women of this country have never had a prime minister who knew the things they know, and the things we know are very different from what men know. . . . Any woman who understands the problems of running a home will be nearer to understanding the problems of running the country.

(*Source:* quoted in Penny Junor, *Margaret Thatcher: Wife, Mother and Politician*, Sidgwick & Jackson, 1983)

Mrs Thatcher has been likened to Elizabeth I. What do you think they have in common?

ON REFLECTION:

What problems are there in using political speeches as historical evidence?

This cartoon depicting Margaret Thatcher as the gangster Al Capone was on the cover of the satirical magazine The Digger *in February 1988.*

PEACE MOVEMENTS

In the twentieth century women have made a significant impact as peace-makers. The following extract is from an article written in the early 1930s by Vera Brittain, a feminist who had served as a nurse in the First World War:

The world today is threatened by the gravest danger that has confronted it since 1914. . . . At such a time of possible catastrophe the part which women might play in the prevention of war becomes a question of special urgency. Men have controlled the world for centuries, yet their civilized ideals are still at the mercy of their primitive impulses. Women, however, represent a new element in politics. . . . Can they, and will they, use this influence to prevent a repetition of that organized slaughter which between 1914 and 1918 destroyed the fine flower of a whole generation?

(*Source:* Vera Brittain "Can the women of the world stop war?", printed in *Modern Woman*, February 1934)

What influence does Vera Brittain believe women can have? Compare this with the views of Lloyd-George and Margaret Thatcher.

The Ulster Peace Movement:

In 1976 two Northern Ireland women, Betty Williams and Mairead Corrigan, were awarded the Nobel Prize for Peace. Following the death of three children when an IRA getaway car went out of control after the driver was shot by a British soldier, these two women went from door to door, asking the women neighbours of the dead children to support them in demonstrating against violence. Two days after the children's death, this report appeared on the front page of the *Sunday Times* newspaper:

More than 10,000 Catholic and Protestant women and children demanding an end to violence in Ulster paraded through the Catholic Andersonstown area of Belfast yesterday . . . the women prayed and sang hymns while a group of IRA youths on a garage roof jeered.

(*Source: Sunday Times*, 15 August 1976)

The Women's Peace Movement gathered strength in Ireland and went on to build community centres to promote reconciliation between Catholics and Protestants. Its power was short-lived, but while it was active, the women's group appeared to have a positive effect in reducing the number of violent deaths in Northern Ireland.

The Greenham Common Peace Camp:

A group of women have been camped permanently beside the perimeter fence of the Greenham Common military base in Berkshire since 1981. They first went there to oppose the building of the American site and the installation of nuclear warheads. Since the arrival of the weapons, they have protested whenever missiles have been taken out on military exercise. The Greenham women are frequently involved in non-violent demonstrations, such as cutting the wire fence or defacing the missile silos

This photograph was taken at Greenham Common in 1982. It shows women taking part in a non-violent blockade of the entry to the missile base. The Greenham Common women have become, to many, a symbol of feminine power.

with peace slogans. Many of them have been arrested for civil disobedience and their camp has been destroyed on a number of occasions. At weekends other women, many of them supporters of the Campaign for Nuclear Disarmament (CND), join the Greenham women to give them support. In December 1982 some 30,000 women converged at Greenham Common to take part in a major demonstration during which they sang and danced and decorated the perimeter fence with symbols of life and peace such as flowers and dove emblems.

Can you suggest reasons why in recent years peace has become a particularly feminine concern?

Looking at evidence from this century, how appropriate are Vera Brittain's comments about women's power?

THE MINERS' STRIKE

In November 1984 women from the Greenham Common Peace Camp joined forces with women from coal-mining communities in a "Mines Not Missiles" rally in York. Many women – miners' wives, mothers and neighbours – played an enormous part in the miners' strike, which lasted from February 1984 to March 1985. Their role included fund-raising, distributing food supplies to the families of striking miners, picketing, appearing on TV, making speeches and organizing support groups. Their involvement and commitment prolonged the strike, and contributed to making it the longest-running national strike in British history. As a consequence of the industrial dispute many working-class women became newly conscious of their power:

Women were awakened to the potential power of the people in grassroots politics. They joined forces with nuclear disarmers in Britain, and after the strike formed an organization with them called "Links". They met regularly and joined cause with black miners in Namibia working in appalling conditions. . . . The women could see that what was happening in the destruction of their pit villages was a microcosm of what was happening in the world at large, where men had almost all the power. The men possessed too little wisdom and were behaving delinquently. Women had hardly any power at all, and there was an uneven spread of world resources. . . . The women of the Third World became their concern too.

(*Source:* Jean Stead, *Never the Same Again: Women and the Miners' Strike*, Women's Press Ltd, 1987)

What points are being made about women by this extract and by the following marching song of the "Sheffield Women Against Pit Closures" Group (SWAPC), written by the mother of a miner?

We can tell the world
We are here to stay
To carry on the struggle
No matter what they say
We can work together
In unity we're strong
So join us in our purpose
And join us in our song

Chorus (x2):
Women marching thru the day
Women working thru the night
Mothers daughters sisters say
Sheffield women fight!

We've been on the picket line
We've been on the dole
We've been on the carpet
But we've reversed our role
We have borne the hardship
We have borne the pain
Now we will bear the battle
And will never be the same.

Chorus (x2)

Women long before us
Have stood up for the right
And more will follow after
To carry on the fight
It never has been easy
And yet we'll struggle on
So join us in our purpose
And join us in our song.

Chorus (x2)

(*Source: The Women's Marching Song* by Iris Preston and Linda Lee Walch)

CURRENT ATTITUDES

Despite the major changes which have taken place this century and such legislation as the 1975 Sex Discrimination Act, many people believe that women are still far from being recognized as equal to men and that power is still largely in male hands. Feminists want to change the patriarchal structures of society, which keep power masculine, and to challenge the belief that control and leadership are male qualities. At the same time, many women neither seek nor want power of a public kind and view female dominance as "unfeminine".

In 1984 a survey of social attitudes in Britain was based on a representative sample of people over 18. The following is an extract:

	% Agree	% Disagree
A wife should avoid earning more than her husband does	14	57
More women should enter politics	52	8
Children are essential for a happy marriage	29	41
Women generally handle positions of responsibility better than men do	22	25
It is wrong for mothers of young children to go out to work	42	32
It should be the woman who decides how many children a couple has	27	42

What do these statistics reveal?

ON REFLECTION:

How useful are surveys of this kind?

What have been the major influences on the relationship between women and power throughout British history?

Glossary

abbess	the senior nun in an abbey, monastery or nunnery
abbot	the senior monk in an abbey, monastery or nunnery
accomplishments	acquired skills such as dancing and playing the piano
Adam	according to the Bible, the first man God created
agrarian	farming- or land-based
anaesthetic	painkilling
Baptists	Protestant sect believing in the baptism of adults only
Beguines	religious women pursuing a devotional life without taking formal monastic vows
benefice	a vicar's duties and the land granted to him as reward
canon	clergyman or monk
capitalism	system of production where an input of capital, or funds, is rewarded by profit
caricature	a representation of someone or something which grotesquely over-emphasizes some feature or trait
chandler	someone who deals in candles, oil, soap and paint
chicory	plant with blue flowers grown for its salad leaves
coalition	a government formed by more than one political party joined together
commonwealth	general welfare of the community
conservative	moderate and opposed to change
contraception	preventing conception and pregnancy
continence	good conduct
contumely	insolent and disgraceful
Crusades	series of Christian expeditions and wars against Islam in the Holy Land
cuckoldry	sexual unfaithfulness by wives, often symbolized by horns
cure of souls	the responsibilities of a vicar for the spiritual welfare of those in his parish
discrimination	unfavourable distinction
dividends	share of profit paid to shareholders
doublet	close-fitting tunic with short skirt, worn by men
drill	repetitive routine
Egyptologist	historian or archaeologist studying Egypt
ell	a length measurement of 45 inches (plural = eln)
emigration	leaving one country to settle in another
enfranchised	given the right to vote
Eve	according to the Bible, the first woman created by God
executor	person appointed to set someone's will into effect
feminist	someone concerned with the cause, rights and qualities of women
femme sole	legal term for single woman, widow, or married woman financially independent from her husband
girdle	belt or cord around the waist
grassroots politics	political activity at a personal or local level
greaves	leg armour
guilds	societies formed by people with a common job or skill, to protect one another's interests
hap	chance to happen
hawks	sells by travelling about

IRA	Irish Republican Army
Levellers	political movement with radical ideals, active at the time of the English Civil War
magnanimity	generosity and graciousness
mantua	woman's loose gown
matriarchy	system of organization of family or society with mother at the head
matricentric	centred around mothers
mead	alcoholic drink made with honey
medieval	from, or of, the Middle Ages
misogynist	someone who hates women
mortality	death rate
Mystics	people of a spiritual or contemplative nature
Nobel Prize	annual award given for outstanding achievement
palisades	fences made of sharp wooden stakes
parishioners	those in the care of a vicar
patriarchy	system of organization of family or society with father as the head
philanthropy	doing "good works" out of a love for people
physick	the art of healing and medicine
picket	line of trade union members formed to dissuade people from working during a strike
piece-work	arrangement where worker is paid according to the number of articles produced rather than for the amount of time worked
Pope	the head of the Roman Catholic Church
post-natal	after the birth of a child
pre-natal	before the birth of a child
prophecy	receiving and communicating messages or pictures from God
Protestant Reformation	major split in the Christian Church in the sixteenth century, resulting in Catholic and Protestant denominations
pseudonym	false or fictitious name of an author
psychology	the study of the mind
Puritans	extreme English Protestants, particularly powerful in the Elizabethan Court
Quakers	Protestant religious group, also called the Society of Friends
quilter	someone who makes quilts
Radical	wanting political reform of a fundamental, root-level kind
rakes	immoral fashionable men
Ranters	fanatical and revolutionary Protestant sect
regiment	government
Restoration	reinstatement of the English monarchy after the Civil War in 1660
retainers	followers
revelations	supernatural revealings of knowledge
rural	concerned with agriculture and the countryside
saloop	a hot drink sold from street stalls as a substitute for coffee
satirical	cynical or sarcastic ridiculing of something
scold	railing or nagging woman
sect	religious body whose views or doctrines differ from those of the orthodox Church
Sessions	the sitting of a legal or judicial assembly
Shakers	religious sect whose name is derived from ecstatic shaking during meetings
shareholders	part-owners of a company and its profits
stereotype	fixed, standard way of viewing or portraying someone
subordinate	subservient to, or under
suffrage	the right to vote in political elections
suffragette	a woman who agitated for suffrage, a member of the WSPU
suffragist	someone who supported women's right to vote

sway	rule or government
temperance	moderation, self-control
Temperance	the movement to restrict and abolish alcoholic drinks
Third World	underdeveloped countries
tippet	a cape or muffler
treatise	an essay on a particular subject
vault	arched roof
vindication	a justification or successful defence of a cause or a person
Virgin Mary	the mother of Christ
vocational	relating to career or occupation
warhead	the explosive section of a nuclear missile
worsted	woollen yarn
writ	official written command

Sources

a review of the types of evidence and sources used in the book

Advertisements

Posters and newspaper advertisements promoting goods, services and ideas are useful sources. The advertisement for Sloane House School (page 33) tells us a lot about women's education in the eighteenth century and the WAAC poster appealing for women workers (page 45) shows that women were called upon to replace men in wartime Britain.

Anthropological evidence

For very early history, where written and archaeological evidence is absent or scarce, the study of the behaviour and ideas of a modern society can give useful clues about the past. Study of the !Kung San peoples in Chapter 1 is an example of this technique. It has obvious limitations because it relies heavily on guesswork.

Archaeological evidence

The excavation of graves, tombs and ancient settlements provides indispensable evidence for historians, particularly before the eleventh century. Artwork, such as the Egyptian tomb painting on page 6, and artefacts like the Anglo-Saxon girdle hanger on page 10, reveal a lot about the lives and values of past societies. People's graves and the articles buried with them can tell us how important or wealthy a person was and give clues about his or her occupation. Objects such as the Scold's Bridle on page 21 give us information about practices and beliefs.

Books and pamphlets

Contemporary books and pamphlets written to inform people or to make a point give valuable information about attitudes and ideas, and their effect on people's lives. This book contains a number of these sources: *The English Housewife* (page 21) contains advice to the seventeenth-century wife; *The Monstrous Regiment of Women* (page 22) attacks female government; and *Sophia* (page 34) makes a point about women's education.

Letters and diaries

Private letters between family members and personal diaries can tell us about the life-styles of people in the past. The Paston Letters (page 13) give a detailed picture of roles and responsibilities within the family; the diary of Florence Nightingale (page 36) shows how many middle-class Victorian women spent their time.

Letters are only written by the educated and literate and diaries are generally kept by people with time to spare, so these sources tend to tell us only about the lives of the wealthier classes.

Literature

Poems, plays and novels are useful sources of information about everyday life as well as indicators of contemporary ideas. The mystery play of *Noah's Flood* (page 11), the poem *Beowulf* (pages 9-10) and the novel *Pamela* (page 32) all reveal current attitudes to women and to the distribution of power.

Newspapers and magazines	Since the eighteenth century newspapers and magazines have been an important source. Most major libraries stock back-copies containing reports, articles, letters and photographs.
Official documents	Wills, tax registers, parish records and Sessions Papers are all important sources of historical evidence. These official papers are particularly useful for finding out people's occupations and the distribution of wealth and power. For example, tax registers from the Middle Ages show that women participated in crafts and trading. Most good reference libraries and county archives will be able to provide these sources.
Oral evidence	This is a valuable additional source of information as it helps us build up a picture of the lives of ordinary people whose testimony is not recorded in written accounts. It is often stored on tape.
Popular songs	Throughout history songs and ballads have been written about events, people and personal feelings. Songs give an interesting insight into the past and into contemporary reactions and ideas. Songs from the Civil War suggest that women fought disguised in both armies. The song on pages 53-54 gives a personal view of the miners' strike.
Rolls of Parliament	These record changes made to the Law such as the Sex Disqualification Act of 1919. They also give information about petitions made to Parliament.
Statistical evidence	The results of censuses and surveys are very useful for historians. They provide information about population, jobs, and, as in the case of the Survey on page 54, people's attitudes.
Written histories and autobiographies	Written histories, such as Tacitus's accounts of the Romans, Bede's *History of the English Church and People* and the *Anglo-Saxon Chronicle*, catalogue many major events and give an insight into the way people thought. What a historian chooses to record reflects what he or she considers to be important. Autobiographies give more personal accounts of the past. As they tend to describe the experiences of only the writer, they deal with a very small sector of history, but this is valuable in building up a wider picture. Autobiographical material is used on pages 19, 36 and 42.

Following on from Women and Power

Here are some topics related to Women and Power which you might like to explore further:

— the history of women's work

— women in religious life

— women in science

— women in the arts

— modern attitudes to women and power

— women in power in other parts of the world

Book List

Interest in women's history has really come to the fore within the last twenty years, with the result that most of the books dealing with women and power are fairly recent and few have been written for young people. The books mentioned here are therefore quite detailed and complex. Many children's history books, however, include short sections on how women lived, and also contain valuable illustrations.

General studies of women and power:

Marilyn French,
Beyond Power: On Women, Men and Morals
Jonathan Cape, 1986

A comprehensive examination of male and female power from prehistoric times to the present day, written from a feminist perspective.

Rosalind Miles,
Women and Power,
Macdonald and Co Ltd, 1985

A lively look at modern women in power in politics, industry and the media.

Sheila Rowbotham,
Hidden from History,
Pluto, 1973

A study of women's powerlessness and their struggle for equality from the sixteenth century to the 1930s.

Books about women in specific periods of history:

Antonia Fraser,
The Weaker Vessel: Woman's Lot in Seventeenth Century England,
Weidenfeld & Nicolson, 1984

An interesting look at the lives of women between the death of Queen Elizabeth and the accession of Queen Anne.

Ivy Pinchbeck,
Women Workers and the Industrial Revolution,
Virago, 1981

A well-documented study of the impact of the agricultural and industrial revolutions on the lives of ordinary women.

Martha Vicinus,
Suffer and Be Still: Women in the Victorian Age,
Indiana University Press, 1972

An exploration of the pressures and changes affecting Victorian women.

Margaret Wade Labarge,
Women in Medieval Life,
Hamish Hamilton, 1986

A fascinating account of medieval women, with numerous excellent illustrations.

Timeline

Notes: **c: (circa)** around about that time   **BC:** Before Christ

PERIOD	DATES	WOMEN'S POWER	WOMEN'S POWERLESSNESS
Prehistoric	**Until 43 AD**	• Possibly high status for women and sexual equality in hunter-gatherer communities	• Possibly reduced status in settled farming communities
Roman	**43 AD to 409 AD**	• Boudica leader of Iceni tribe • Boudica's daughters heirs to royal line • Female leadership accepted by Tacitus as normal	
Anglo-Saxon	**409-1066**	• Noblewomen own, inherit and dispose of lands • Wealthy women have high status • Abbesses control prestigious mixed-sex monasteries	• Female servants buried alive on death of mistress
Middle Ages	**1066-1500**	• Widows allowed to own property • Wealthy women have domestic and economic power as household managers • Women active in crafts and trades and in farming • Power of midwives feared by the Christian Church • Writings and prophesying of religious women and Mystics influential	• Many girls married by their families in their early teens • Married women have no legal rights • Wife-beating common • Women excluded from many guilds • Church restricting practice of female midwifery • Double monasteries close and nunneries decline as centres of learning
Sixteenth and Seventeenth Centuries	**1500-1700**	• Puritans oppose wife-beating and stress spiritual equality • Elizabeth I's reign regarded as exceptional for her sex • Women active and influential during Civil War • Religious sects permit women to participate and preach • Women crucial to Britain's textile trade	• Obedience expected from married women • Women denied positions of control in Church, politics and society • Women's increased power and influence in Civil War suppressed with Restoration of monarchy • Lives of upper-class women geared increasingly to leisure and idleness • Lack of education for girls • Guilds increasingly exclude women

AD: (Anno Domini) In the Year of Our Lord   Century: a hundred years

ADDITIONAL POINTS	SIGNIFICANT EVENTS
• Insufficient evidence to draw any conclusions about women's power	**c. 4500 BC** Britain becomes an island **c. 3500 BC** Farming develops **c. 1700 BC** First metal artefacts **1490-68 BC** Hatshepsut Pharoah in Egypt **c. 700 BC** Iron Age
• Insufficient evidence to draw any general conclusions about women's power	**43 AD** Roman invasion of Britain **50** Foundation of London **61** Iceni Revolt **410** End of Roman rule in Britain
• Little evidence of the lives of poorer women	**597** St Augustine's mission to bring Christianity to England **664** Synod of Whitby **793 onwards** Viking attacks and invasions
• Women stereotyped as saints or scolds in contemporary art and literature	**1066** Norman Conquest **1086** Domesday survey **1095** The first of the Crusades **1139-53** Period of civil war in England **1215** Magna Carta **1315** Great Famine **1348** Black Death **1381** The Peasants' Revolt **1400** Death of Chaucer **1485** Death of Richard III at Battle of Bosworth Field Accession of Henry (VII) Tudor **1486** Malleus Malificarum **1492** Columbus reaches the West Indies
• Married women spend a large proportion of their lives bearing children • Widespread speculation in educated circles about women's roles	**1536** Dissolution of Monasteries **1558** Accession of Elizabeth I **1588** Defeat of Spanish Armada **1594** Start of series of bad harvests **1603** Death of Elizabeth I **1616** Death of Shakespeare **1642** Start of the Civil War **1649-60** The Commonwealth and Protectorate **1665** Great Plague **1666** Fire of London

Timeline

PERIOD	DATES	WOMEN'S POWER	WOMEN'S POWERLESSNESS
Eighteenth century	1700-1800	• Farmer's wives run dairies • Women active in agricultural improvements	• Wife-beating still common • Universities and professions closed to women • Women denied leadership in the Church • Wives of gentry and upper classes become idle, leisured consumers • Poor women employed as cheap labour in factories • Women's pay lower than men's
Nineteenth century	1800-1900	• Queen Victoria reigns for most of century • Significant changes to marriage and property laws in 1880s and 1890s • First girls' secondary schools and women's colleges established • Teaching, clerical and nursing professions opened to women • Women active in trade unions • Middle-class women administer charity organizations	• Women denied leadership in the Church • Prostitution common among working-class women and girls • Women factory workers employed in poor conditions for low wages • Middle-class women restricted by pressures of "respectability"
Twentieth century	1900 onwards	• Significant breakthroughs in industry and the professions • Legal changes to raise status of women and give equal rights • Increased availability of birth control • Women replacing men in work during both wars • Women taking on traditionally male roles of leadership, e.g. in politics • Women active in trade unions and peace protesting • Women in mining communities prolong the miners' strike	• Women receiving lower wages than men for similar jobs • Few women MPs or Cabinet Ministers • High incidence of rape and sexual attack on women

AD: (Anno Domini) In the Year of Our Lord   **Century:** a hundred years

ADDITIONAL POINTS	SIGNIFICANT EVENTS
• The feminine ideal influences upper classes and the wives of wealthy farmers who aspire to leisured living • Novels present women as virtuous, passive and dependent • Marriage increasingly love-based • More emphasis on the family unit	**1707** Union of England and Scotland **1769** James Watt steam engine patented **1776** Declaration of American Independence **1789** French Revolution **1792** "Vindication of the Rights of Women"
• Feminine ideal continues to influence the middle classes • Improved plumbing and household appliances • Some improvements in pre- and post-natal care • Chloroform discovered as pain relief for childbirth (1847) • Development of contraceptive devices	**1801** Union with Ireland **1815** Battle of Waterloo and end of French Wars **1825** Stockton & Darlington Railway opens **1837** Accession of Queen Victoria **1859** Darwin publishes *'Origin of Species'* **1888** Bryant & May match-girls' strike
• 1950s development of the Pill • Crèches provided from 1920s onwards	**1901** Death of Queen Victoria **1914-18** First World War **1918** Women over 30 allowed to vote **1919** First woman sits in Parliament **1926** General Strike **1928** All women over 21 allowed to vote **1939-45** Second World War **1973** Britain enters the EEC **1979** Margaret Thatcher becomes Prime Minister **1984-85** Miners' strike

Index